Basic Digital Logic Design

PREFACE

➢ ABOUT BOOK:

This book covers many basic digital logic design theoretical exercises and practical laboratory experiments. These are helpful for BCA, MCA, B.Sc and M.Sc (Electronics, Computer Science), BE and M.Tech (Electronics, Computer Science) degree students.

Usually the practical approach to digital logic design needs a hardware called Integrated Circuit(IC) trainer kit. The absence of this hardware can be filled by using any software simulators available in the technology market. One such simple free simulator we are using here is called "LOGISIM" (**LOGI**c **SIM**ulator) which can be installed on Windows, macOS, or Linux operating systems and used for designing the digital logic circuits.

The Logisim software is used most often by students in computer science classes to design and experiment with digital circuits in simulation. Circuits are designed in Logisim using a graphical user interface similar to traditional drawing programs, an interface also found in many other simulators. Unlike most other simulators of Logisim's sophistication, Logisim allows the user to edit the circuit during simulation. The relative simplicity of the interface makes it work well for survey courses. Design features for more sophisticated circuits, such as the "subcircuits" and "wire bundles" found in Logisim, are available in few other open-source graphical tools.

While users can design complete CPU implementations within Logisim, the software is designed primarily for educational use. Professionals typically design such large-scale circuits using a hardware description language such as Verilog or VHDL. Logisim is unable to accommodate analog components.

➢ ABOUT AUTHOR:

Pen name: KSS

Education: BE; M.Tech(CSE)

Designation: Assistant Professor

Experience: 8 years+

INDEX

CHAPTER 1: Digital Logic Exercises

1. Convert the following decimal numbers to binary, octal and hexadecimal numbers showing the steps clearly
   (i) 155.53   (ii) 444.44   (iii) 1039.48   (iv) 999.99

2. Convert the following binary numbers to decimal, octal and hexadecimal
   (i) 1110110110001.111   (ii) 110100011.101   (iii) 1111.11   (iv) 11001100.01

3. Perform the following conversions:

   (i)   (101010111100)BCD = ( )Ex-3
   (ii) (333)8 = ( )2
   (iii) (-178)10 = ( )2 in 2's complement
   (iv) (225)10 = ( )2 in 2's complement

4. Assume an 8-bit register to store numbers in signed magnitude representation. Find the 1's and 2's complement of the following fixed-point numbers.
   (i) -23   (ii) 0   (iii) -76   (iv) 65

5. Add the following numbers in 8-bit register using signed 2's complement representation.
   (i) +50 and −5   (ii) +45 and −65   (iii) +75 and +85   (iv) -46 and -46. Also indicate the overflow if any.

6. Reduce the following expression using Boolean algebra.
   (i)   XYZ(XY + Z' (YZ + XZ))
   (ii)   XZ(X'YZ + XY + Z)
   (iii) ABEF + AB(EF)' + A'B + EF
   (iv)   AB + (AC)' + AB'C (AB + C)
   (v)   ABC + ABC' + A'B
   (vi)   B'D + A'BC' + ACD + A'BC
   (vii) ABC (A'B + BBC)
   (viii) A (B + C' (AB + AC')')

7. Without reducing, implement the following expression in AOI logic and then convert into NAND logic.

   (i) $F(x,y,z) = \sum(2,3,4,7)$

8. Realize the following Boolean functions using multilevel NAND / NOR logic

   (i) y = AB' + A (B + C)(A + B')
   (ii) y = A' + B'C + BC' (A + B)
   (iii) y = (A + B' + C)(B' + C) + A'C

9. Express the following functions in sum of minterms and product of maxterms.

   (i) F(x,y,z) = (x' + y)(y' + z)

   (ii) F (A,B,C,D) = A'B'D + ABD' + C'D + ABC'

10. Obtain simplified expression in SOP form
    (i) x'z' + y'z' + yz' + xyz

11. Obtain simplified expression in POS form

    (i) (A + B + D') (A' + B + D) (C + D) (C' + D')

12. Simplify the Boolean function F defined by

    $F(W,X,Y,Z) = \sum(1,3,7,11,15) + \sum d (0,2,5)$

13. Verify Demorgan's theorem for three variables using truth table.

14. A 4 input logic circuit have output high for decimal equivalent values 0, 1, 4, 7, 8, 9 and has don't care condition for decimal equivalent values 2, 3, 5, 11, 10. Remaining Outputs are low. Write standard SOP from Boolean equation for above. Simplify this equation using K-map and realize it with NOR gates only.

15. Design combinational circuit that converts a decimal digit from 8, 4, -2, - 1 code to BCD.

16. Design a digital circuit which gives an output equal to '1' when a valid BCD is applied to it as an input , otherwise output is '0'.

17. Design a full adder logic circuit and implement the same using only NAND gates.

18. Design and implement a full subtractor using 4:1 Multiplexers.

19. Design a 3-bit binary counter using T-flip-flops.

20. Design and implement a BCD Ripple Counter.

CHAPTER 2 : Experiments Performed On IC Digital Trainer Kit

1. Realization of basic gates.
2. Realization of Universal gates.
3. Realization of SOP expression using universal gates.
4. Realization of POS expression using universal gates.
5. Design half and full adder using NAND gate.
6. Design half and full subtractor using NAND gate.
7. Realization of parallel adder/ subtractor using IC and XOR gate.
8. Realization of code conversion from BCD to Ex-3 and vice versa.
9. Realization of code conversion from Gray to Binary and vice versa.
10. Realization of 1-bit and 2-bit comparator using IC-7485.
11. Realization of odd and even parity generation and checking.

CAPTER 1: DIGITAL LOGIC EXERCISES

1: Convert the following decimal numbers to binary, octal and hexadecimal numbers showing the steps clearly
   (i) 155.53   (ii) 444.44   (iii) 1039.48   (iv) 999.99

SOLUTION:

> ### DECIMAL NUMBERS TO BINARY CONVERSION:-

Conversion method:

A) Convert the integral part of decimal to binary equivalent

1. Divide the decimal number by 2 and store remainders in array.
2. Divide the quotient by 2.
3. Repeat step 2 until we get the quotient equal to zero.
4. Equivalent binary number would be reverse of all remainders of step 1.

B) Convert the fractional part of decimal to binary equivalent

1. Multiply the fractional decimal number by 2.
2. Integral part of resultant decimal number will be first digit of fraction binary number.
3. Repeat step 1 using only fractional part of decimal number and then step 2.
4. Repeat these step3 till you get 6 places (or the precision you wish) to the right of the radix.

C) Combine both integral and fractional part of binary number.

(i) 155.53

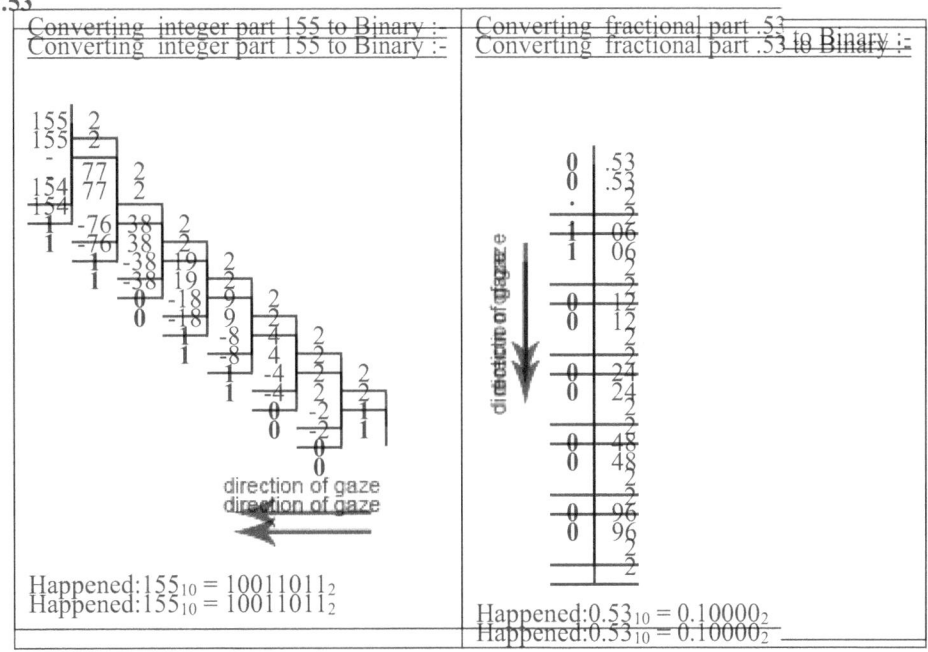

Happened: $155_{10} = 10011011_2$

Happened: $0.53_{10} = 0.10000_2$

Add up together whole and fractional part here so: $10011011_2 + 0.10000_2 = 10011011.10000_2$
Result of converting:- $155.53_{10} = 10011011.10000_2$

(ii) 444.44

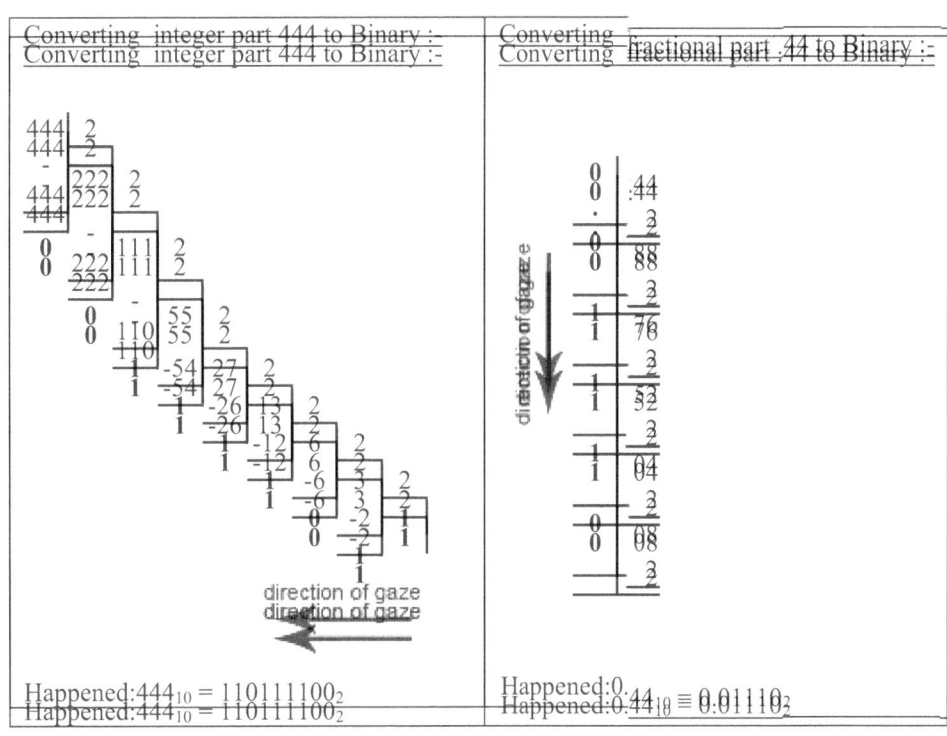

Happened: $444_{10} = 110111100_2$

Happened: $0.44_{10} \equiv 0.01110_2$

Add up together whole and fractional part here so: $110111100_2 + 0.01110_2 = 110111100.01110_2$
Result of converting:- $444.44_{10} = 110111100.01110_2$

(iii) 1039.48

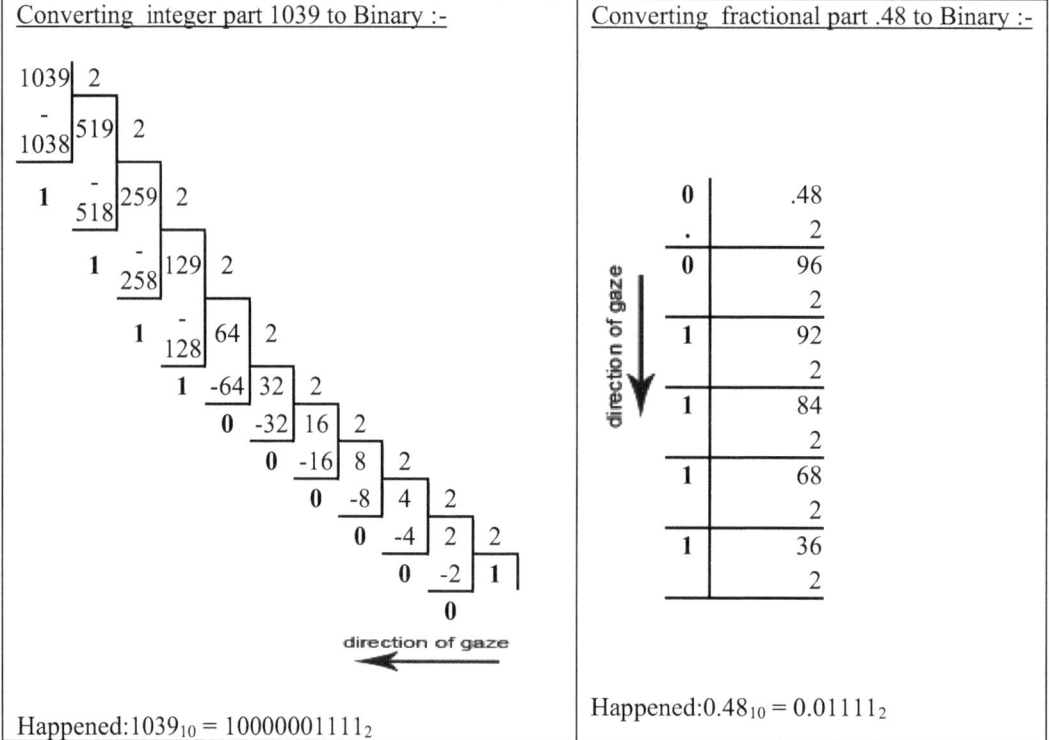

Add up together whole and fractional part here so: $10000001111_2 + 0.01111_2 = 10000001111.01111_2$
Result of converting:- **$1039.48_{10} = 10000001111.01111_2$**

(iv) 999.99

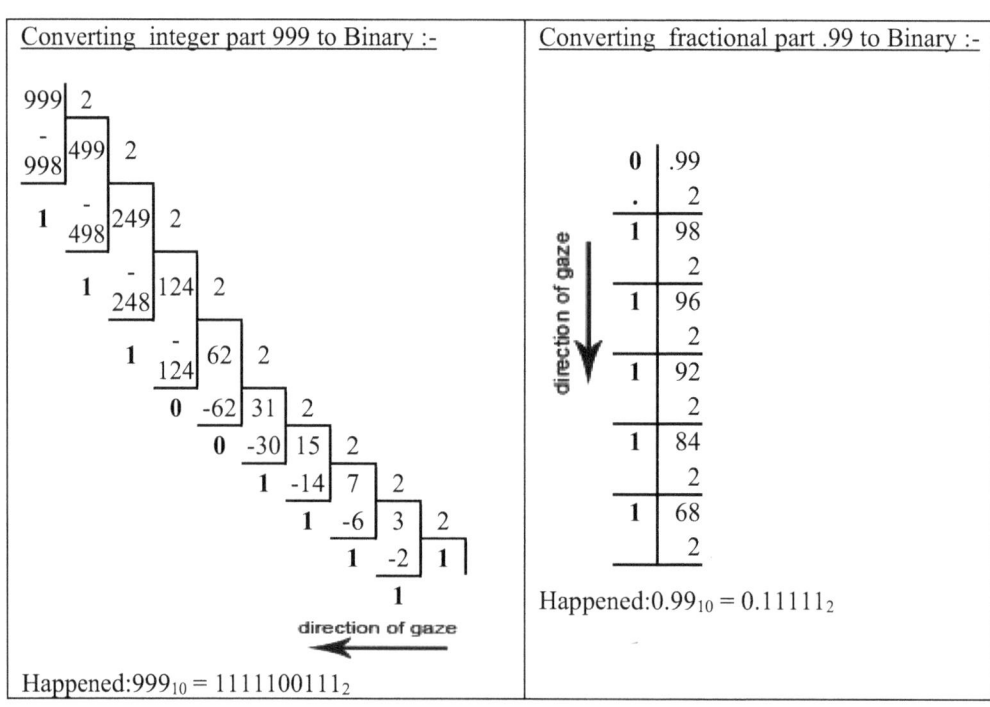

Add up together whole and fractional part here so: $1111100111_2 + 0.11111_2 = 1111100111.11111_2$
Result of converting:- **$999.99_{10} = 1111100111.11111_2$**

➤ DECIMAL NUMBERS TO OCTAL CONVERSION:-

Conversion method: Follow the same above conversion method here also but take the base as 8.

(i) 155.53

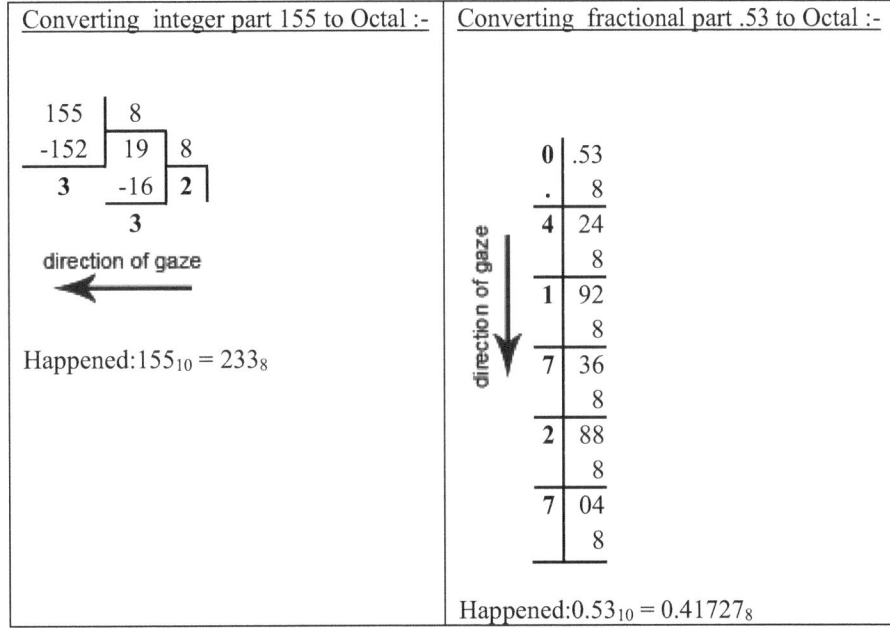

Converting integer part 155 to Octal :-	Converting fractional part .53 to Octal :-

155 | 8
-152 | 19 | 8
  3 | -16 | 2
         | 3
direction of gaze ←
 	
Happened: $155_{10} = 233_8$
	0 | .53
	  | 8
	4 | 24
	  | 8
	1 | 92
	  | 8
	7 | 36
	  | 8
	2 | 88
	  | 8
	7 | 04
	  | 8
	direction of gaze ↓
	
	Happened: $0.53_{10} = 0.41727_8$

Add up together whole and fractional part here so: $233_8 + 0.41727_8 = 233.41727_8$
Result of converting:- **$155.53_{10} = 233.41727_8$**

(ii) 444.44

Converting integer part 444 to Octal :-	Converting fractional part .44 to Octal :-

444 | 8
-440 | 55 | 8
  4 | -48 | 6
        | 7
direction of gaze ←
 	
Happened: $444_{10} = 674_8$
	0 | .44
	  | 8
	3 | 52
	  | 8
	4 | 16
	  | 8
	1 | 28
	  | 8
	2 | 24
	  | 8
	1 | 92
	  | 8
	direction of gaze ↓
	
	Happened: $0.44_{10} = 0.34121_8$

Add up together whole and fractional part here so: $674_8 + 0.34121_8 = 674.34121_8$
Result of converting:- **$444.44_{10} = 674.34121_8$**

(iii) 1039.48

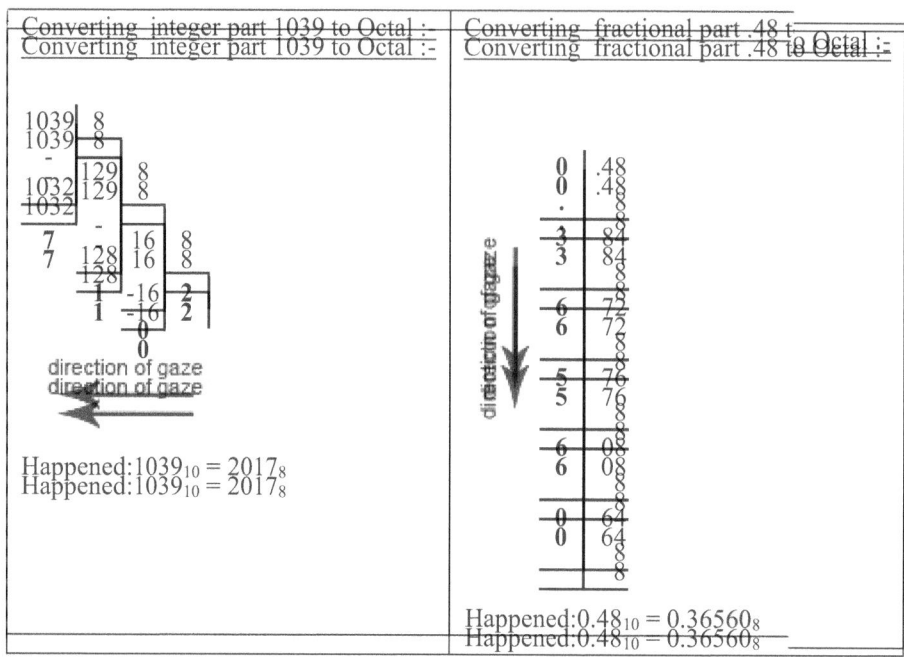

Add up together whole and fractional part here so: $2017_8 + 0.36560_8 = 2017.36560_8$

Result of converting:- $1039.48_{10} = 2017.36560_8$

(iv) 999.99

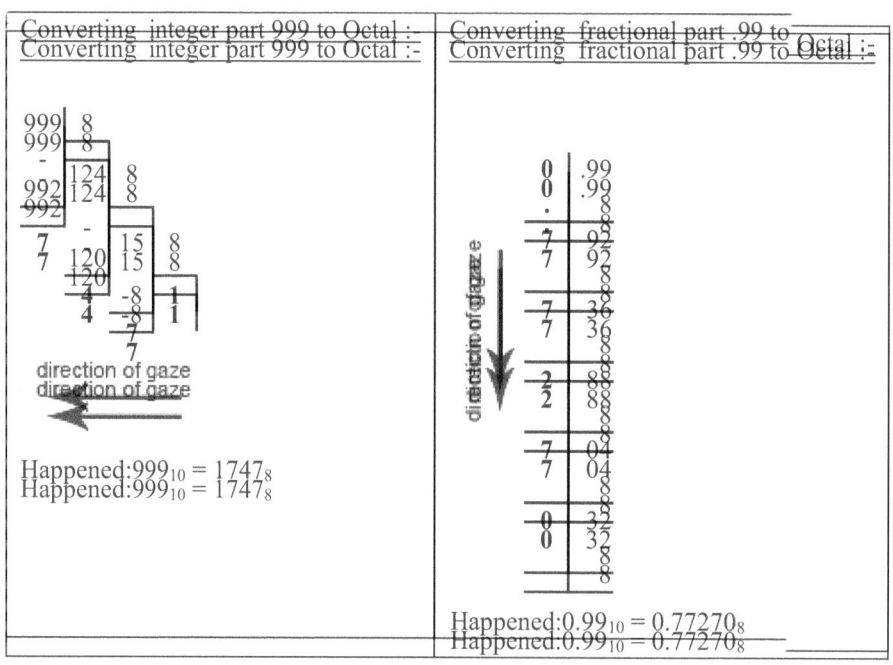

Add up together whole and fractional part here so: $1747_8 + 0.77270_8 = 1747.77270_8$

Result of converting:- $999.99_{10} = 1747.77270_8$

➢ DECIMAL NUMBERS TO HEXADECIMAL CONVERSION:-

Conversion method: Follow the same above conversion method here also but take the base as 16:

(i) **155.53**

Converting integer part 155 to Hexadecimal :-	Converting fractional part .53 to Hexadecimal :-
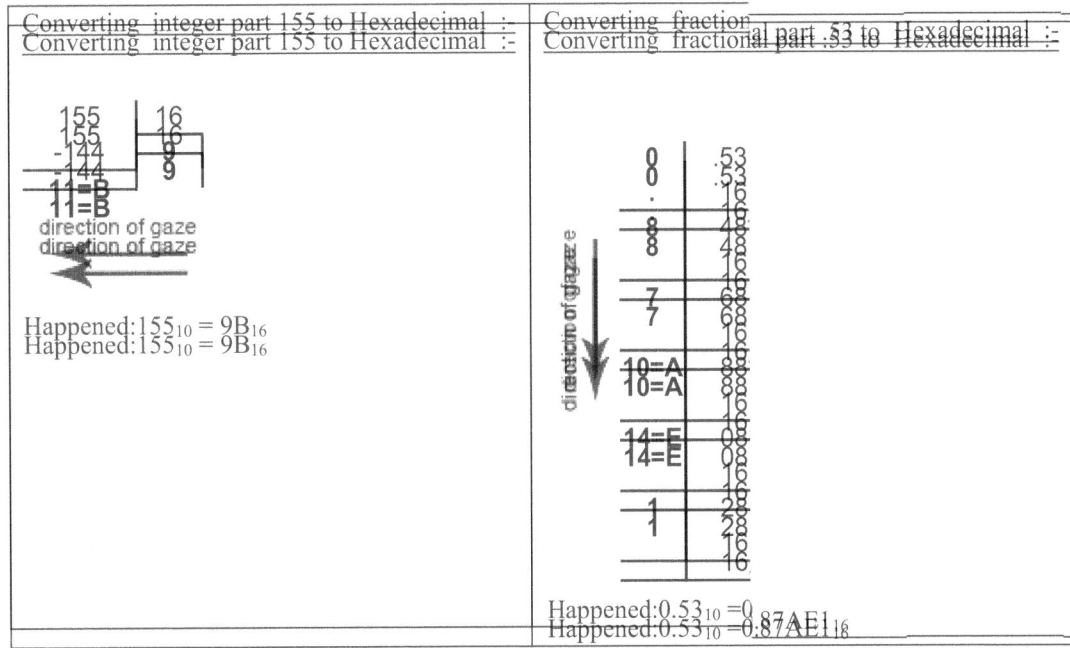	

Happened: $155_{10} = 9B_{16}$

Happened: $0.53_{10} = 0.87AE1_{16}$

Add up together whole and fractional part here so: $9B_{16} + 0.87AE1_{16} = 9B.87AE1_{16}$

Result of converting:- $155.53_{10} = 9B.87AE1_{16}$

(ii) **444.44**

Converting integer part 444 to Hexadecimal :-	Converting fractional part .44 to Hexadecimal :-
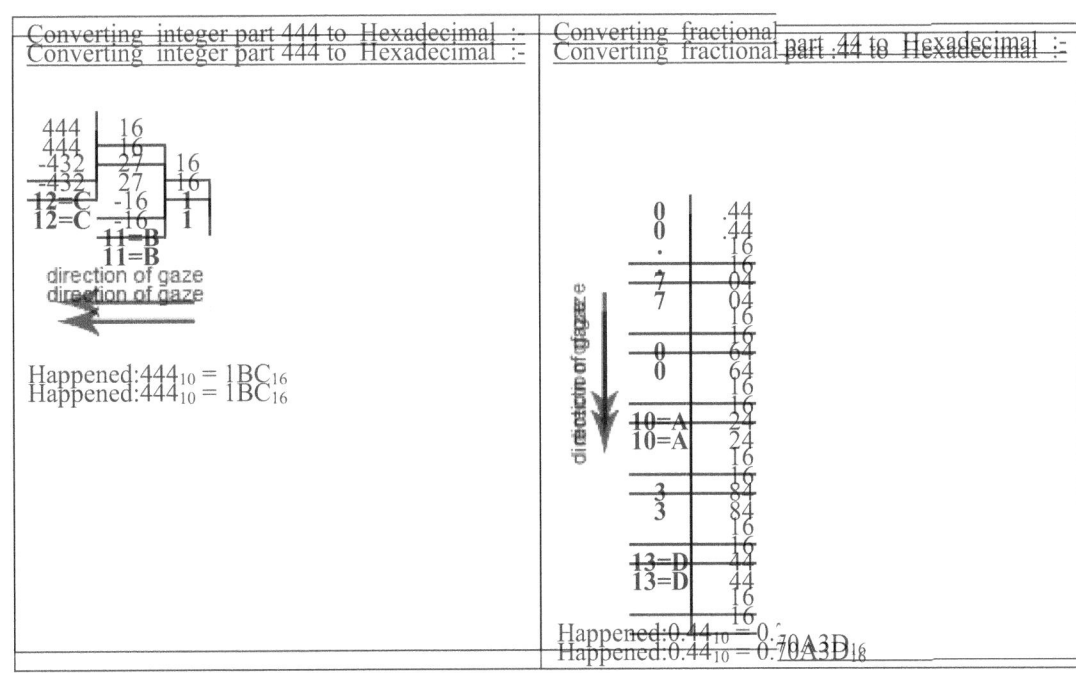	

Happened: $444_{10} = 1BC_{16}$

Happened: $0.44_{10} = 0.70A3D_{16}$

Add up together whole and fractional part here so: $1BC_{16} + 0.70A3D_{16} = 1BC.70A3D_{16}$

Result of converting:- $444.44_{10} = 1BC.70A3D_{16}$

(iii) 1039.48

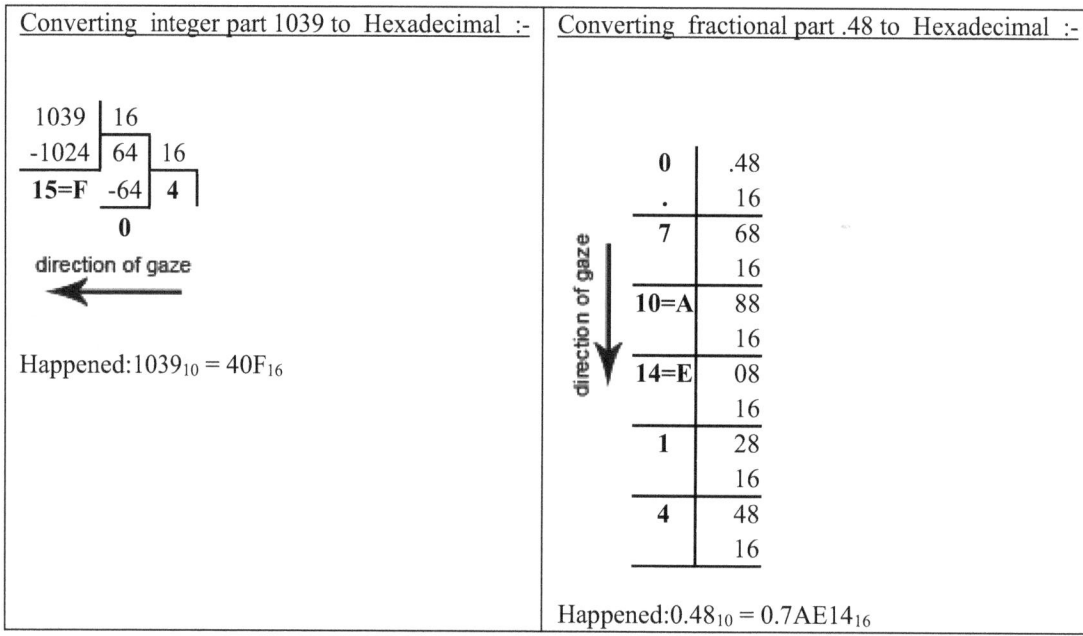

Add up together whole and fractional part here so: $40F_{16} + 0.7AE14_{16} = 40F.7AE14_{16}$
Result of converting:- **$1039.48_{10} = 40F.7AE14_{16}$**

(iv) 999.99

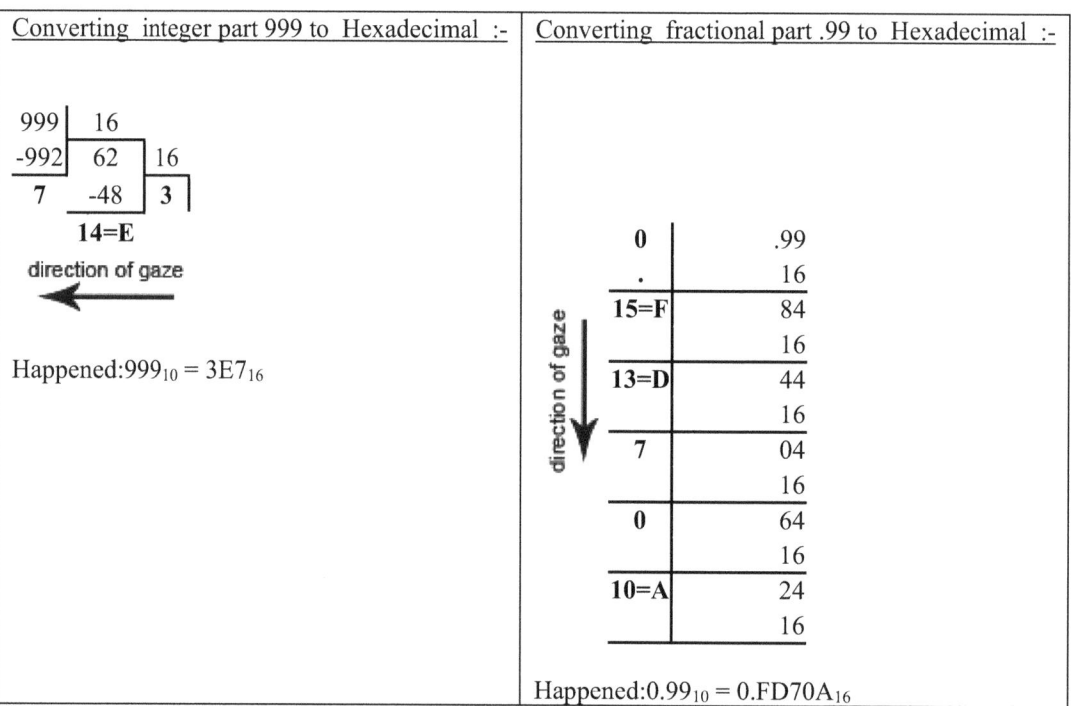

Add up together whole and fractional part here so: $3E7_{16} + 0.FD70A_{16} = 3E7.FD70A_{16}$
Result of converting:- **$999.99_{10} = 3E7.FD70A_{16}$**

2. Convert the following binary numbers to decimal, octal and hexadecimal
(i) 111011011001.111 (ii) 110100011.101 (iii) 1111.11 (iv) 11001100.01

SOLUTION:

> **BINARY NUMBERS TO DECIMAL CONVERSION:-**

Conversion method: Expand the number given in binary form in the power of 2 and sum the values, the result which we will get will be in the decimal form.

(i) 111011011001.111

111011011001.111_2

$= 1·2^{11}+1·2^{10}+1·2^{9}+0·2^{8}+1·2^{7}+1·2^{6}+0·2^{5}+1·2^{4}+1·2^{3}+0·2^{2}+0·2^{1}+1·2^{0}+1·2^{-1}+1·2^{-2}+1·2^{-3}$

$= 2048+1024+512+0+128+64+0+16+8+0+0+1+0.5+0.25+0.125$

$= 3801.875_{10}$

Result of converting: $111011011001.111_2 = 3801.875_{10}$

(ii) 110100011.101

110100011.101_2

$= 1·2^{8}+1·2^{7}+0·2^{6}+1·2^{5}+0·2^{4}+0·2^{3}+0·2^{2}+1·2^{1}+1·2^{0}+1·2^{-1}+0·2^{-2}+1·2^{-3}$

$= 256+128+0+32+0+0+0+2+1+0.5+0+0.125$

$= 419.625_{10}$

Result of converting: $110100011.101_2 = 419.625_{10}$

(iii) 1111.11

1111.11_2

$= 1·2^{3}+1·2^{2}+1·2^{1}+1·2^{0}+1·2^{-1}+1·2^{-2}$

$= 8+4+2+1+0.5+0.25$

$= 15.75_{10}$

Result of converting: $1111.11_2 = 15.75_{10}$

(iv) 11001100.01

11001100.01_2

$= 1·2^{7}+1·2^{6}+0·2^{5}+0·2^{4}+1·2^{3}+1·2^{2}+0·2^{1}+0·2^{0}+0·2^{-1}+1·2^{-2}$

$= 128+64+0+0+8+4+0+0+0+0.25$

$= 204.25_{10}$

Result of converting: $11001100.01_2 = 204.25_{10}$

➢ BINARY NUMBERS TO OCTAL CONVERSION:-

Conversion method:

Step 1 = Divide the binary digits into groups of three (starting from the right).

Step 2 = Convert each group of three binary digits to one octal digit.

Binary number	Octal number conversion	Result
$(111011011001.111)_2$	111 011 011 001 . 111 7_8 3_8 3_8 1_8 7_8	$(7331.7)_8$
$(110100011.101)_2$	110 100 011 . 101 6_8 4_8 3_8 5_8	$(643.5)_8$
$(1111.11)_2$	001 111 . 110 1_8 7_8 6_8	$(17.6)_8$
$(11001100.01)_2$	011 001 100 . 010 3_8 1_8 4_8 2_8	$(314.2)_8$

➢ BINARY NUMBERS TO HEXADECIMAL CONVERSION:-

Conversion method:

Step 1 = Divide the binary digits into groups of four (starting from the right).

Step 2 = Convert each group of four binary digits to one hexadecimal symbol.

Binary number	Hexadecimal number conversion	Result
$(111011011001.111)_2$	1110 1101 1001 . 1110 E B 9 E	$(EB9.E)_{16}$
$(110100011.101)_2$	0001 1010 0011 . 1010 1 A 3 A	$(1A3.A)_{16}$
$(1111.11)_2$	1111 . 1100 F C	$(F.C)_{16}$
$(11001100.01)_2$	1100 1100 . 0100 C C 4	$(CC.4)_{16}$

3. Perform the following conversions.

(i) $(101010111100)_{BCD} = (\quad)_{Ex-3}$
(ii) $(333)_8 = (\quad)_2$
(iii) $(-178)_{10} = (\quad)_2$ in 2's complement
(iv) $(225)_{10} = (\quad)_2$ in 2's complement

SOLUTION:

(i) $(101010111100)_{BCD} = (\quad)_{Ex-3}$

BCD to Ex-3 code conversion:-

The truth table for the conversion is given below. The X's mark don't care conditions.

BCD(8421)				Excess-3			
A	B	C	D	W	X	Y	Z
0	0	0	0	0	0	1	1
0	0	0	1	0	1	0	0
0	0	1	0	0	1	0	1
0	0	1	1	0	1	1	0
0	1	0	0	0	1	1	1
0	1	0	1	1	0	0	0
0	1	1	0	1	0	0	1
0	1	1	1	1	0	1	0
1	0	0	0	1	0	1	1
1	0	0	1	1	1	0	0
1	0	1	0	X	X	X	X
1	0	1	1	X	X	X	X
1	1	0	0	X	X	X	X
1	1	0	1	X	X	X	X
1	1	1	0	X	X	X	X
1	1	1	1	X	X	X	X

$(1010\ 1011\ 1100)_{BCD} = (XXXX\ XXXX\ XXXX)_?$

Result: Given 101010111100 number is not a valid BCD number, therefore it can not be converted to any number.

(ii) $(333)_8 = (\quad)_2$

Step 1 = Convert each octal digit to a 3-digit binary number (the octal digits may be treated as decimal for this conversion).

Step 2 = Combine all the resulting binary groups (of 3 digits each) into a single binary number.

Octal number	Binary number conversion			Result
$(333)_8$	3_{10} $(011)_2$	3_{10} $(011)_2$	3_{10} $(011)_2$	$(011011011)_2$

(iii) $(-178)_{10} = (\ )_2$ in 2's complement   (iv) $(225)_{10} = (\ )_2$ in 2's complement

No.	Binary number conversion	1's complement representation (Inverse the Binary code only for negative number)	2's complement representation (Add 1 to 1's complement representation only for negative number)
-178	178 ÷ 2 = 89 r 0 89 ÷ 2 = 44 r 1 44 ÷ 2 = 22 r 0 22 ÷ 2 = 11 r 0 11 ÷ 2 = 5 r 1 5 ÷ 2 = 2 r 1 2 ÷ 2 = 1 r 0 1 ÷ 2 = 0 r 1 direction of gaze ← <u>Result of converting:</u> $178_{10} = 10110010_2$	01001101	01001101 + 1 ----------- 01001110 **<u>1</u>01001110** ↓ Indicates that it is a -ve number Therefore <u>Result of converting:</u> $-178_{10} = 101001110_2$
225	225 ÷ 2 = 112 r 1 112 ÷ 2 = 56 r 0 56 ÷ 2 = 28 r 0 28 ÷ 2 = 14 r 0 14 ÷ 2 = 7 r 0 7 ÷ 2 = 3 r 1 3 ÷ 2 = 1 r 1 1 ÷ 2 = 0 r 1 direction of gaze ← <u>Result of converting:</u> $225_{10} = 11100001_2$	011100001	**<u>0</u>11100001** ↓ Indicates that it is a +ve number Therefore <u>Result of converting:</u> $225_{10} = 011100001_2$

4. Assume an 8-bit register to store numbers in signed magnitude representation. Find the 1's and 2's complement of the following fixed-point numbers.

(i) -23 (ii) 0 (iii) -76 (iv) 65

SOLUTION:

No.	Binary code	1's complement representation (Inverse the Binary code only for negative number)	2's complement representation (Add 1 to 1's complement representation only for negative number)
-23	**Result of converting:** $23_{10} = 10111_2$ **8-bit representation:** 00010111	11101000	11101000 + 1 --------------- 11101001
0	00000000	00000000	00000000
-76	**Result of converting:** $76_{10} = 1001100_2$ **8-bit representation:** 01001100	10110011	10110011 + 1 --------------- 10110100
65	**Result of converting:** $65_{10} = 1000001_2$ **8-bit representation:** 01000001	01000001	01000001

5. Add the following numbers in 8-bit register using signed 2's complement representation:

(i) +50 and −5 (ii) +45 and −65 (iii) +75 and +85 (iv) −46 and −46. Also indicate the overflow if any.

SOLUTION:

(i) +50 and −5

Number	Binary code	2's complement representation	Addition result
+50	00110010	00110010	00110010 + 11111011 -------- 1 00101101 ↳ +ve sign overflow Result = +45 in decimal
−5	00000101	11111010 → 1's complement + 1 -------- 11111011	

(ii) +45 and −65

Number	Binary code	2's complement representation	Addition result
+45	00101101	00101101	00101101 + 10111111 -------- 11101100 ↳ −ve sign Result = −20 in decimal
−65	01000001	10111110 → 1's complement + 1 -------- 10111111	

(iii)   +75 and +85

Number	Binary code	2's complement representation	Addition result
+75	01001011	01001011	01001011 + 01010101 ----------- 10100000 Result:- Overflow = not enough binary digits to display this value (If 9-bit register is used then 010100000 = +160 in decimal)
+85	01010101	01010101	

(iv)   -46 and -46

Number	Binary code	2's complement representation	Addition result
-46	00101110	11010001 → 1's complement + 1 ----------- 11010010	11010010 + 11010010 ----------- 1 10100100 ↓ ↳ -ve sign overflow Result ≡ -92 in decimal
-46	00101110	11010001 → 1's complement + 1 ----------- 11010010	

6. Reduce the following expression using Boolean algebra.

    (i)   XYZ(XY + Z' (YZ + XZ))
    (ii)   XZ (X'YZ + XY + Z)
    (iii)   ABEF + AB(EF)' + A'B + EF
    (iv)   AB + (AC)' + AB'C (AB + C)
    (v)   ABC + ABC' + A'B
    (vi)   B'D + A'BC' + ACD + A'BC
    (vii) ABC (A'B + BBC)
    (viii) A (B + C' (AB + AC')')

SOLUTION:

(i) **XYZ(XY + Z' (YZ + XZ))**
   = XYZ (XY) + XYZ (Z' (YZ + XZ))
   = XXYYZ + XYZ (YZZ' + XZZ')
   = XYZ + XYZ (0)   --→Since A.A=A and A.A'=0
   = XYZ

(ii) **XZ (X'YZ + XY + Z)**
   = XZ (X'YZ) + XZ (XY) + XZ(Z)
   = XX'YZZ + XXYZ + XZ Z
   = (0)YZZ + XYZ + XZ   --→Since A.A=A and A.A'=0
   = XZ(Y + 1)
   = XZ   --→Since A+1=1

(iii) **ABEF + AB(EF)' + A'B + EF**
   = AB(EF +(EF)') + A'B + EF
   = AB + A'B + EF   -→Since A+A'=1
   = B(A + A') + EF
   = B + EF   -→Since A+A'=1

(iv) **AB + (AC)' + AB'C (AB + C)**
   = AB + (AC)' + AB'C (AB + C)
   = AB + (AC)' + AABB'C +AB'CC
   = AB + (AC)' + 0+AB'C   --→Since A.A=A and A.A'=0
   =A(B+B'C) + (AC)'
   =A((B+B'). (B+C)) + (AC)'   --→Since Distributive law B+(B'C)= (B+B'). (B+C)
   =A(B+C) + (AC)'   -→Since A+A'=1
   =AB +AC + (AC)'
   =AB + 1   -→Since A+A'=1
   =1   --→Since A+1=1

(v) ABC + ABC' + A'B
=AB(C + C') + A'B
=AB + A'B   →Since   A+A'=1
=B (A+ A')
=B   →Since   A+A'=1

(vi)   B'D + A'BC' + ACD + A'BC
= B'D + A'B(C'+C) + ACD
= B'D + A'B + ACD   →Since   A+A'=1

(vii)   ABC (A'B + BBC)
= ABC (A'B + BC)   --→Since   A.A=A
= AA'BBC + ABBCC
= **0** + ABC   --→Since   A.A=A and A.A'=0
= ABC

(viii)   A (B + C' (AB + AC')')

= A (B + C' ((AB)'. (AC')'))   --→Since (A+B)'=A'.B'

= A (B + C'((A'+B') (A'+C)))   --→Since (A.B)'=A'+B'

= A (B + C' (A'A'+A'C+A'B'+B'C))

= A (B + C' (A'A'+A'C+A'B'+B'C))

= A (B + C' (A'+A'C+A'B'+B'C))   --→Since   A.A=A

= A (B + A'C'+A'CC'+A'B'C'+B'CC')

= A (B + A'C'+0+A'B'C'+0)   --→Since   A.A'=0

= AB +AA'C'+AA'B'C'

= AB   --→Since   A.A'=0

7. Without reducing, implement the following expressions in AOI logic and then convert into NAND logic.

(i) $F(x,y,z) = \Sigma(2,3,4,7)$

SOLUTION:

The Karnaugh map for the above given function can be written as follows:

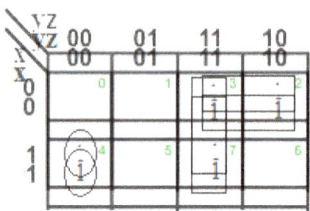

From the above Karnaugh map function can be simplified as follows:

$$F = \bar{x}y + yz + x\bar{y}\bar{z}$$

➢ IMPLEMENTATION IN AOI LOGIC:-

AOI logic:- It is a combinational logic design implemented with AND gates, OR gates and INVERTER gates.

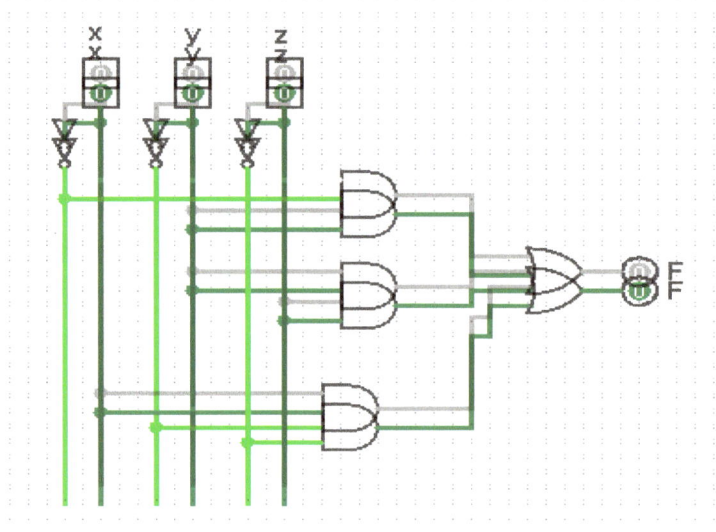

➢ CONVERSION INTO NAND LOGIC:-

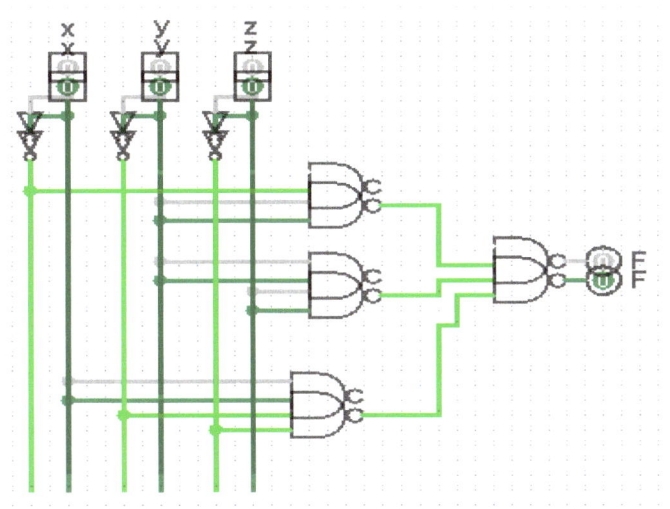

8. Realize the following Boolean functions using multilevel NAND / NOR logic

(i) y = AB' + A (B + C)(A + B')
(ii) y = A' + B'C + BC' (A + B)
(iii) y = (A + B' + C)(B' + C) + A'C

SOLUTION:

(i)   y = AB' + A (B + C)(A + B')

Let us simplify the above Boolean function as given below:

y = AB' + A (B + C)(A + B')
  = AB' + (A B + AC) (A + B')

  = AB' + $\underline{A\ B\ A}$ + AB B' + $\underline{ACA}$ + ACB'

  = AB' + A B + 0 + AC + ACB'   ---> Since A.A=A and A.A'=0
  = A(B' + B) + AC + AB'C

  = A + AC + AB'C   ---> Since A+A'=1

$\boxed{y = A + AC + AB'C}$

> **REALIZATION USING NAND LOGIC :-**

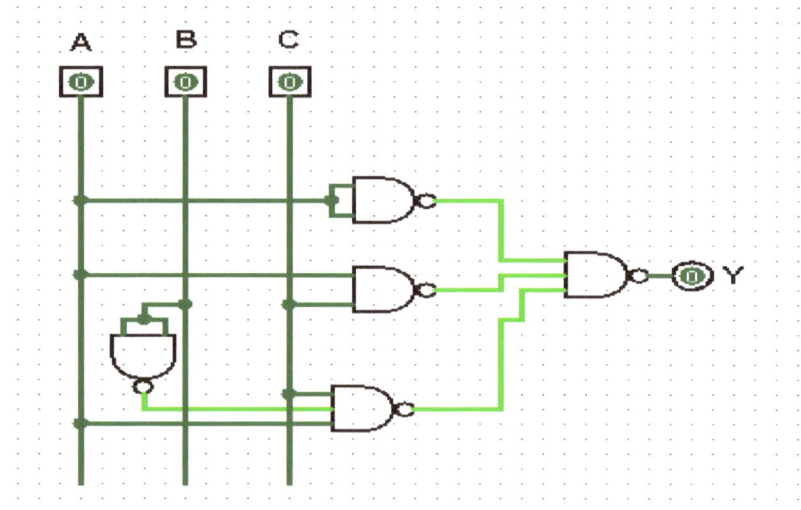

24

(ii) y = A' + B'C + BC' (A + B)

Let us simplify the above Boolean function as given below:

y = A' + B'C + BC' (A + B)

  = A' + B'C + BC'A + BC'B
  = A' + B'C + ABC' + <u>BC'B</u>
  = A' + B'C + <u>ABC' + BC'</u>   --->Since A.A=A
  = A' + B'C + BC'(A + 1)
  = A' + B'C + BC'   --->Since A+1=1

$$\boxed{y = A' + B'C + BC'}$$

- ### REALIZATION USING NAND LOGIC :-

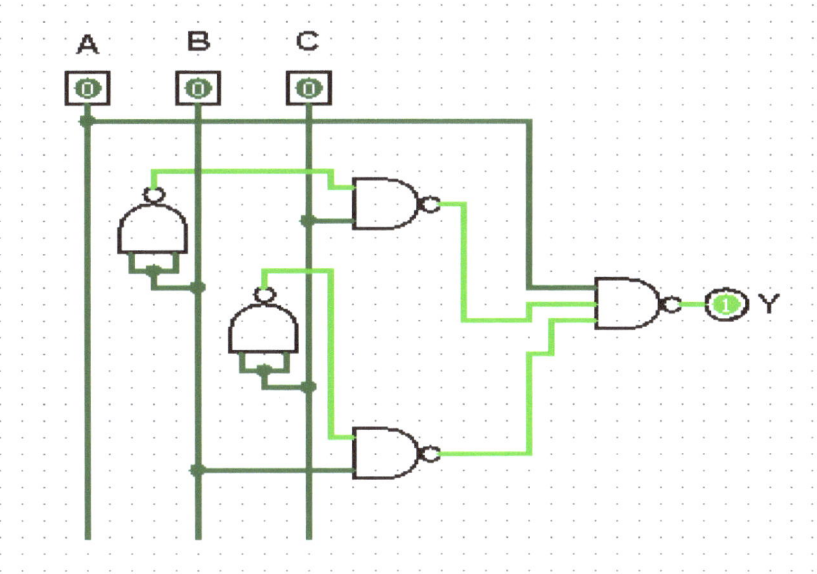

(iii) $y \equiv (A + B' + C)(B' + C) + A'C$

Let us simplify the above Boolean function as given below:

$y \equiv (A + B' + C)(B' + C) + A'C$

$\equiv (AB' + B'B' + CB') + (AC + B'C + CC) + A'C$
$\equiv AB' + B' + B'C + AC + B'C + C + A'C$ ---> Since A.A=A
$\equiv B'(A + 1) + B'C + C(A+1) + A'C$ ---> Since A+1=1
$\equiv B' + B'C + C + A'C$
$\equiv B'(1 + C) + C + A'C$
$\equiv B' + C + A'C$ ---> Since A+1=1

$$\boxed{y \equiv B' + C + A'C}$$

> ### REALIZATION USING NAND LOGIC :-

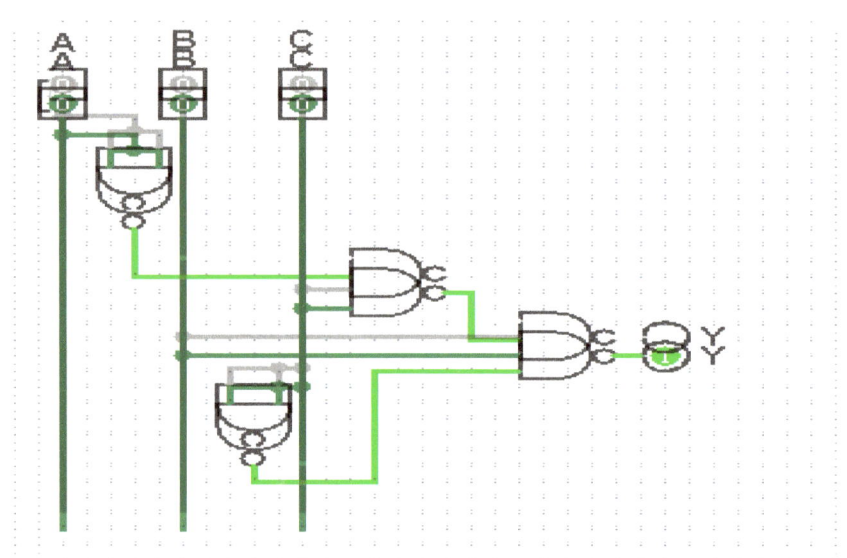

9. Express the following functions in sum of minterms and product of maxterms:

(i) $F(x,y,z) = (x' + y)(y' + z)$

(ii) $F(A,B,C,D) = A'B'D + ABD' + C'D + ABC'$

SOLUTION:

(i) $F(x,y,z) = (x' + y)(y' + z)$

Sum of minterms:

$F(x,y,z) = x'y' + x'z + yy' + yz$

$= x'y'(z+z') + x'z(y+y') + 0 + yz(x+x')$ ---> Since $A \cdot A' \equiv 0$

$= x'y'z + x'y'z' + x'yz + x'y'z + xyz + x'yz$

It can be re-written as:

$= x'y'z + x'y'z + x'y'z' + x'yz + x'yz + xyz$

$= x'y'z + x'y'z' + x'yz + xyz$ ---> Since $A + A \equiv A$

It can be written in Sum of minterms as:

$$\sum m(0, 1, 3, 7)$$

Product of maxterms:

$F(x,y,z) = (x' + y)(y' + z)$
$= (x' + y)(z \cdot z')(y' + z)(x \cdot x')$
$= (x' + y + z)(x' + y + z')(x + y' + z)(x' + y' + z)$

It can be written in Product of maxterms as:

$$\prod M(1, 2, 3, 5)$$

(ii)   F (A,B,C,D) = A'B'D + ABD' + C'D + ABC'

Sum of minterms:

F (A,B,C,D) = A'B'D + ABD' + C'D + ABC'

= A'B'D(C+C') + ABD'(C+C') + C'D(A+A')(B+B') + ABC'(D+D')

= A'B'CD + <u>A'B'C'D</u> + ABCD' + <u>ABC'D'</u> + <u>ABC'D</u> + <u>A'B'C'D</u> + <u>ABC'D</u> + <u>ABC'D'</u>

= A'B'CD + A'B'C'D + ABCD' + ABC'D' + ABC'D   --->Since A+A=A

It can be written in Sum of minterms as :

$$\sum m (1,3,12,13,14)$$

Product of maxterms:

F (A,B,C,D) = A'B'D + ABD' + C'D + ABC'

Write the above given SOP form expression into POS form as:

F (A,B,C,D) = (A'+B'+D) (A+B+D') (C'+D) (A+B+C')

= (A'+B'+D) (C.C')
  (A+B+D') (C.C')
  (C'+D) (A.A')(B.B')
  (A+B+C')(D.D')

=(A'+B'+C+D) <u>(A'+B'+C'+D)</u>
  (A+B+C+D') <u>(A+B+C'+D')</u>
  <u>(A+B+C'+D)</u> <u>(A'+B'+C'+D)</u>
  <u>(A+B+C'+D)</u> <u>(A+B+C'+D')</u>

=(A'+B'+C+D) (A'+B'+C'+D)
  (A+B+C+D') (A+B+C'+D')
  (A+B+C'+D)   --->Since A+A=A

It can be written in Product of maxterms as :

$$\pi M (1,3,12,13,14)$$

10. Obtain simplified expression in SOP form
    (i) x'z' + y'z' + yz' + xyz

SOLUTION:

The above SOP form can be written as :

x'z' + y'z' + yz' + xyz = x'z'(y+y') + y'z'(x+x') + yz'(x+x') + xyz   → Since A+A'=1

        = x'y z'+ x'y'z'+ x y'z' + x'y'z' + xyz' + x'yz' + xyz

    It can be re-written as

        = x'y z'+ x'y z'+ x'y'z'+ xyz + x y'z' + xyz'

        = x'y z' + x'y'z'+ xyz + x y'z' + xyz'   → Since A+A=A

It can be written in Sum of minterms as :

$$\sum m\,(0, 2, 4, 6, 7)$$

---

11. Obtain simplified expression in POS form
    (i) (A + B + D') (A' + B + D) (C + D) (C' + D')

SOLUTION:

The above POS form can be written as :

(A + B + D') (A' + B + D) (C + D) (C' + D')

    = (A + B + D'+ C . C') (A' + B + D + C . C') (C + D + A . A'+ B . B') (C' + D' + A . A'+ B . B')

    = (A + B + C+ D') (A + B + C'+ D') (A' + B + C+ D) (A' + B + C'+ D) (A + B + C+ D) (A' + B' + C+ D) (A + B + C'+ D') (A' + B' + C'+ D')

    = (A + B + C+ D') (A + B + C'+ D') (A' + B + C+ D) (A' + B + C'+ D) (A + B + C+ D) (A' + B' + C+ D) (A' + B' + C'+ D')   → Since A+A=A

It can be written in Product of maxterms as :

$$\pi M\,(0, 3, 5, 7, 12, 14, 15)$$

12: Simplify the Boolean function F defined by

$$F(W;X;Y;Z) = \sum(1,3,7,11,15) + \sum_d(0,2,5)$$

SOLUTION:

The Karnaugh map for the above given function can be written as follows:

AB\CD	00	01	11	10
00	X	1	1	X
01		X	1	
11			1	
10			1	

From the above Karnaugh map function can be simplified as follows:

$$F = \bar{A}B + CB$$

13: Verify DeMorgan's theorem for three variables using truth table.

De Morgan's theorem can be stated as follows:-

Theorem 1:

The compliment of the product of two variables is equal to the sum of the compliment of each variable.

Thus according to De-Morgan's theorem if A, B and C are the three variables or Boolean numbers then it can be written that:

$$(A.B.C)' = A' + B' + C'$$

> **TRUTH TABLE:-**

A	B	C	(A.B.C)'	A'	B'	C'	A'+B'+C'
0	0	0	1	1	1	1	1
0	0	1	1	1	1	0	1
0	1	0	1	1	0	1	1
0	1	1	1	1	0	0	1
1	0	0	1	0	1	1	1
1	0	1	1	0	1	0	1
1	1	0	1	0	0	1	1
1	1	1	0	0	0	0	0

Theorem 2:

The compliment of the sum of two variables is equal to the product of the compliment of each variable.

Thus according to De Morgan's theorem if A, B and C are the three variables or Boolean numbers then it can be written that:

$$(A+B+C)' = A'.B'.C'$$

> **TRUTH TABLE:-**

A	B	C	(A+B+C)'	A'	B'	C'	A'.B'.C'
0	0	0	1	1	1	1	1
0	0	1	0	1	1	0	0
0	1	0	0	1	0	1	0
0	1	1	0	1	0	0	0
1	0	0	0	0	1	1	0
1	0	1	0	0	1	0	0
1	1	0	0	0	0	1	0
1	1	1	0	0	0	0	0

14. A 4 input logic circuit have output high for decimal equivalent values 0, 1, 4, 7, 8, 9 and has don't care condition for decimal equivalent values 2, 3, 5, 11, 10. Remaining Outputs are low. Write standard SOP from Boolean equation for above. Simplify this equation using K-map and realize it with NOR gates only.

SOLUTION:

The SOP from Boolean equation for the given logic circuit is:
$F(A,B,C,D) = \sum m(0,1,4,7,8,9) + \sum d(2,3,5,11,10)$.

AB \ CD	00	01	11	10
00	1 (0)	1 (1)	X (3)	X (2)
01	1 (4)	X (5)	1 (7)	0 (6)
11	0 (12)	0 (13)	0 (15)	0 (14)
10	1 (8)	1 (9)	X (11)	X (10)

The simplified Boolean expression is $F = \overline{A}\,\overline{C} + \overline{A}\,D + A\,\overline{B}$

The above Boolean expression is F is realized using only NOR gates as given in the following circuit diagram:

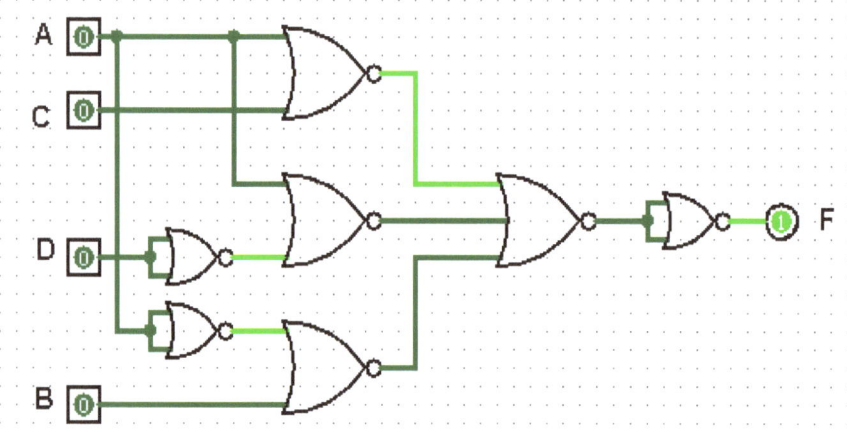

15. Design combinational circuit that converts a decimal digit from 8, 4, -2, - 1 code to BCD.

SOLUTION:

> **TRUTH TABLE:-**

	INPUTS				OUTPUTS			
	8	4	-2	-1	8	4	2	1
	A	B	C	D	w	x	y	z
0	0	0	0	0	0	0	0	0
1	0	1	1	1	0	0	0	1
2	0	1	1	0	0	0	1	0
3	0	1	0	1	0	0	1	1
4	0	1	0	0	0	1	0	0
5	1	0	1	1	0	1	0	1
6	1	0	1	0	0	1	1	0
7	1	0	0	1	0	1	1	1
8	1	0	0	0	1	0	0	0
9	1	1	1	1	1	0	0	1

> **KARNAUGH MAPS:-**

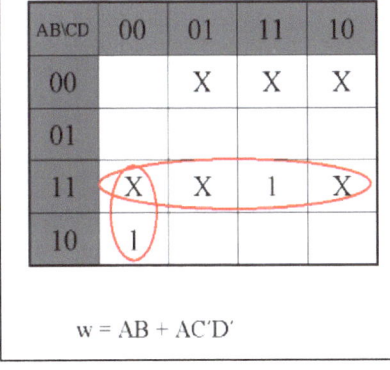

$w = AB + AC'D'$

$x = B'C + B'D + BC'D'$

$y = C'D + CD'$

and $z = D$

COMBINATIONAL CIRCUIT DIAGRAM:-

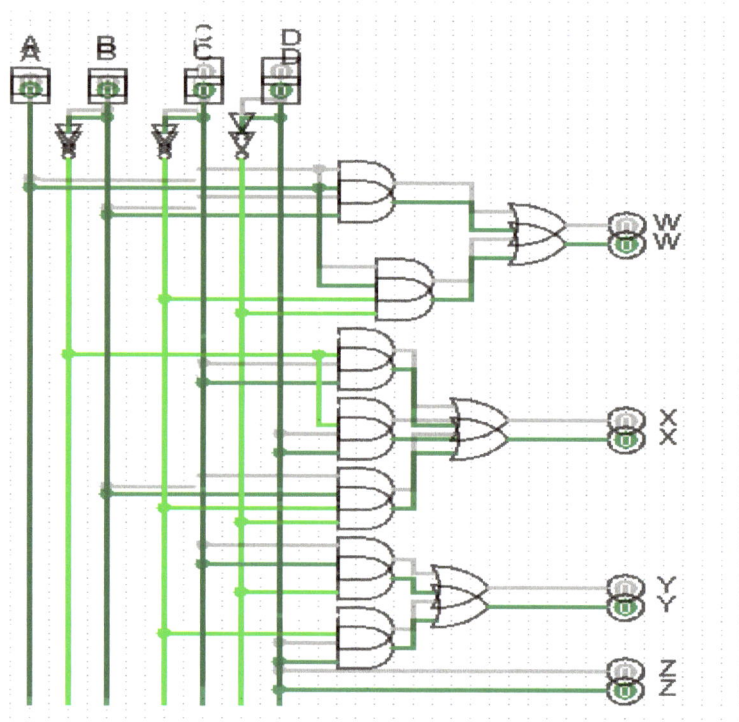

16. Design a digital circuit which gives an output equal to '1' when a valid BCD is applied to it as an input; otherwise output is '0'.

SOLUTION:

> **TRUTH TABLE:-**

A	B	C	D	Y	
0	0	0	0	1	
0	0	0	1	1	
0	0	1	0	1	
0	0	1	1	1	Valid BCD
0	1	0	0	1	
0	1	0	1	1	
0	1	1	0	1	
0	1	1	1	1	
1	0	0	0	1	
1	0	0	1	1	
1	0	1	0	0	
1	0	1	1	0	
1	1	0	0	0	Invalid BCD
1	1	0	1	0	
1	1	1	0	0	
1	1	1	1	0	

> **KARNAUGH MAP:-**

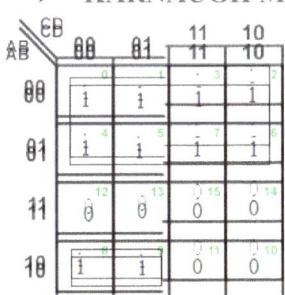

The simplified Boolean expression is $Y = \overline{A} + \overline{A}\,\overline{B}\,\overline{C}$

> **LOGIC DIAGRAM:-**

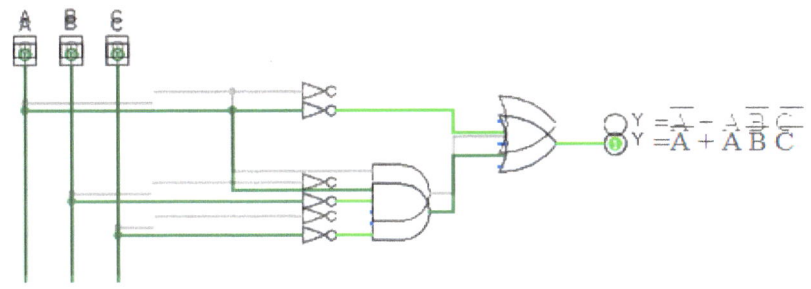

17. Design a full adder logic circuit and implement the same using only NAND gates.

THEORY:

Full-Adder:
The half-adder does not take the carry bit from its previous stage into account. This carry bit from its previous stage is called carry-in bit. A combinational logic circuit that adds two data bits, A and B, and a carry-in bit, Cin, is called a full-adder.

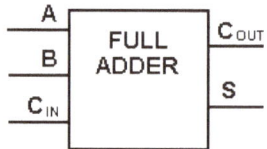

(1) Designing FULL ADDER logic circuit:-

> **TRUTH TABLE:-**

INPUTS			OUTPUTS	
A	B	Cin	S	C
0	0	0	0	0
0	0	1	1	0
0	1	0	1	0
0	1	1	0	1
1	0	0	1	0
1	0	1	0	1
1	1	0	0	1
1	1	1	1	1

> **KARNAUGH MAPS:-**

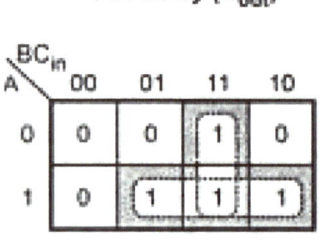

$C_{out} = AB + A\,C_{in} + B\,C_{in}$

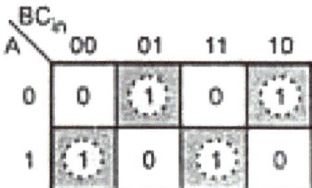

$Sum = \overline{A}\,\overline{B}C_{in} + \overline{A}B\overline{C}_{in} + A\overline{B}\,\overline{C}_{in} + ABC_{in}$

$$\begin{aligned}
\text{Sum} &= \bar{A}\,\bar{B}\,C_{in} + \bar{A}\,B\,\bar{C}_{in} + A\,\bar{B}\,\bar{C}_{in} + A\,B\,C_{in} \\
&= C_{in}\,(\bar{A}\,\bar{B} + AB) + \bar{C}_{in}\,(\bar{A}\,B + A\,\bar{B}) \\
&= C_{in}\,(A \odot B) + \bar{C}_{in}\,(A \oplus B) \\
&= C_{in}\,(\overline{A \oplus B}) + \bar{C}_{in}\,(A \oplus B) \\
&= C_{in} \oplus (A \oplus B)
\end{aligned}$$

i.e., Sum = A $\oplus$ B $\oplus$ C_{in}

> **LOGIC DIAGRAM:-**

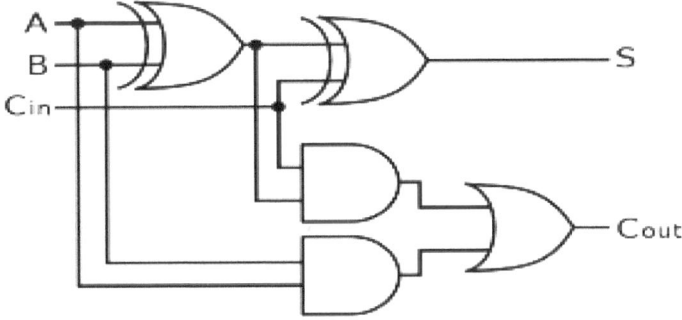

(2) Implementing the FULL ADDER using only NAND gates:-

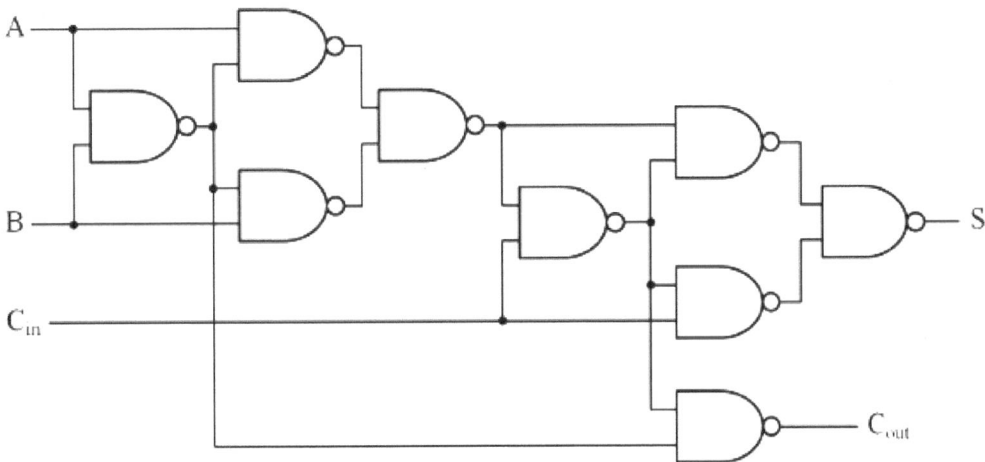

18: Design and implement a full subtractor using 4:1 Multiplexers.

THEORY:

Full Subtractor:

Subtracting two single-bit binary values, B, C_{in} from a single-bit value A (i.e., $A - (B$ and $B_{in})$) produces a difference bit D and a borrow out B_{Out} bit. This is called full subtraction.

(1) Designing FULL SUBTRACTOR logic circuit:-

➢ **TRUTH TABLE:-**

Inputs			Outputs	
A	B	B_{in}	D	B_{out}
0	0	0	0	0
0	0	1	1	1
0	1	0	1	1
0	1	1	0	1
1	0	0	1	0
1	0	1	0	0
1	1	0	0	0
1	1	1	1	1

➢ **LOGIC DIAGRAM OF FULL SUBTRACTOR:-**

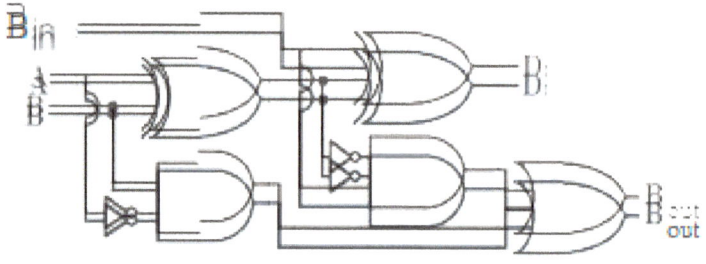

(2) Implementing the FULL SUBTRACTOR using 4:1 Multiplexers:

4:1 Multiplexer:

A 4-to-1 multiplexer consists four data input lines as D0 to D3, two select lines as S0 and S1 and a single output line Y. The select lines S1 and S2 select one of the four input lines to connect the output line. The particular input combination on select lines selects one of input (D0 through D3) to the output. The figure (a) below shows the block diagram of a 4-to-1 multiplexer in which the multiplexer decodes the input through select line.

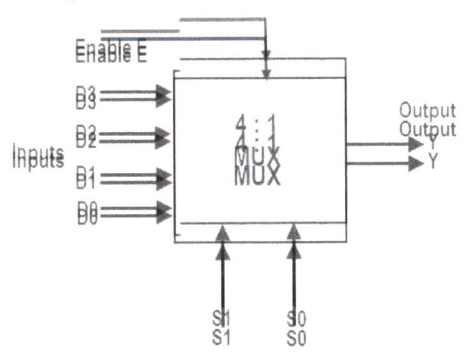

(a) Block diagram (b) Truth table

The truth table of a 4-to-1 multiplexer is shown above in figure (b) where four input combinations 00, 10, 01 and 11 on the select lines respectively switches the inputs D0, D2, D1 and D3 to the output. That means when S1=0 and S0=0, the output at Y is D0; similarly Y is D1 if the select inputs S1=0 and S0=1 and so on.

The following figure (c) shows the logic circuits for implementing the full subtractor using 4:1 multiplexers. Both Difference and Borrow are implemented separately by cascading two 4:1 multiplexers and one 2:1 multiplexer. Since there are 3 inputs in the full subtractor's truth table, we need two 4:1 multiplexers and one 2:1 multiplexer to have 3 select lines as A, B and B_{in}.

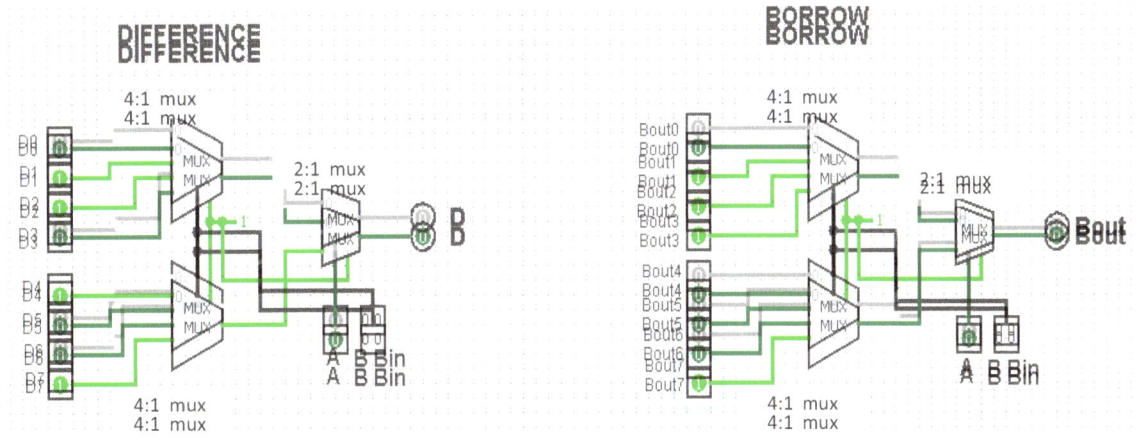

(c) Logic circuits for implementing the full subtractor using 4:1 Multiplexers

19. Design a 3-bit binary counter using T-flip-flops.

THEORY:

3-BIT BINARY COUNTER :

A counter is nothing more than a specialized register or pattern generator that produces a specified output pattern or sequence of binary values (or states) upon the application of an input pulse signal called the "Clock".

The clock is actually used for data transfer in these applications. Typically, counters are logic circuits that can increment or decrement a count by one but when used as asynchronous divide-by-n counters they are able to divide these input pulses producing a clock division signal.

Counters are formed by connecting flip-flops together and any number of flip-flops can be connected or "cascaded" together to form a "divide-by-n" binary counter where "n" is the number of counter stages used and which is called the **Modulus**. The modulus or simply "MOD" of a counter is the number of output states the counter goes through before returning itself back to zero, i.e., one complete cycle.

In 3-bit binary counter the three flip-flops will count from 0 to 7 i.e., 2^n-1. It has eight different output states representing the decimal numbers 0 to 7 and is called a **Modulo-8** or **MOD-8** counter. A counter with four flip-flops will count from 0 to 15 and is therefore called a **Modulo-16** counter and so on.

An example of this is given as follows:

- 3-bit Binary Counter = 2^3 = 8 (modulo-8 or MOD-8)

➢ TRUTH TABLE:-

Output State Transitions		Flip-flop inputs
Present State Q2 Q1 Q0	Next State Q2 Q1 Q0	T2 T1 T0
0 0 0	0 0 1	0 0 1
0 0 1	0 1 0	0 1 1
0 1 0	0 1 1	0 0 1
0 1 1	1 0 0	1 1 1
1 0 0	1 0 1	0 0 1
1 0 1	1 1 0	0 1 1
1 1 0	1 1 1	0 0 1
1 1 1	0 0 0	1 1 1

➢ STATE DIAGRAM OF A 3-BIT BINARY COUNTER:-

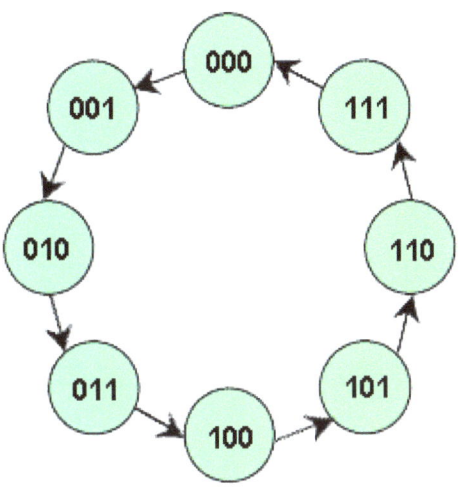

➢ LOGIC DIAGRAM :-

The following diagram shows the design of a 3-bit binary counter using 3 T-flip-flops FF0, FF1 and FF2 having 3 inputs as T0,T1 and T2 with Q0,Q1 and Q2 as outputs respectively. All the 3 flip flops are connected to a common input clock signal Clk ,by changing which we get different outputs as given in the above truth table.

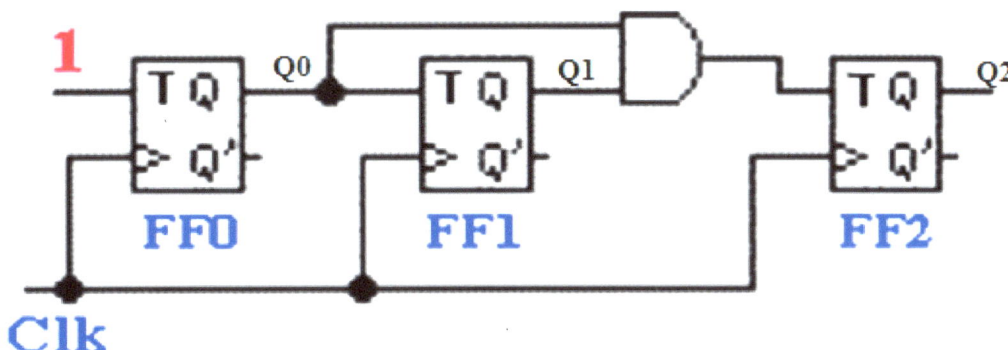

20: Design and implement a BCD Ripple Counter.

THEORY:

BCD Ripple Counter :

- This counter follows a sequence of 10 states and returns to 0 after the count of 9. Such a counter must have at least **four flip-flops** to represent each decimal digit since a decimal digit is represented by a binary code with at least four bits.
- The logic diagram of a BCD ripple counter using JK flip-flops has four outputs which are designated by the letter symbol Q with a numeric subscript equal to the binary weight of the corresponding bit in the BCD code.
- The output of Q_1 is applied to the C inputs of both Q_2 and Q_8 and the output of Q_2 is applied to the C input of Q_4.
- The J and K inputs are connected either to a permanent 1 signal or to outputs of other flip-flops.

- **Flip-Flop transitions:**

    - Q_1 changes state after each clock pulse.
    - Q_2 complements every time Q_1 goes from 1 to 0 as long as $Q_8 = 0$. When Q_8 becomes 1 Q_2 remains at 0.
    - Q_4 complements every time Q_2 goes from 1 to 0.
    - Q_8 remains at 0 as long as Q_2 or Q_4 is 0. When both Q_2 and Q_4 become 1, Q_8 complements when Q_1 goes from 1 to 0. Q_8 is cleared on the next transition of Q_1.

➢ TRUTH TABLE:-

Clock Count	Output bit Pattern				Decimal Value
	Q_8	Q_4	Q_2	Q_1	
1	0	0	0	0	0
2	0	0	0	1	1
3	0	0	1	0	2
4	0	0	1	1	3
5	0	1	0	0	4
6	0	1	0	1	5
7	0	1	1	0	6
8	0	1	1	1	7
9	1	0	0	0	8
10	1	0	0	1	9
11	Counter Resets its Outputs back to Zero				

STATE DIAGRAM OF A BCD RIPPLE COUNTER:-

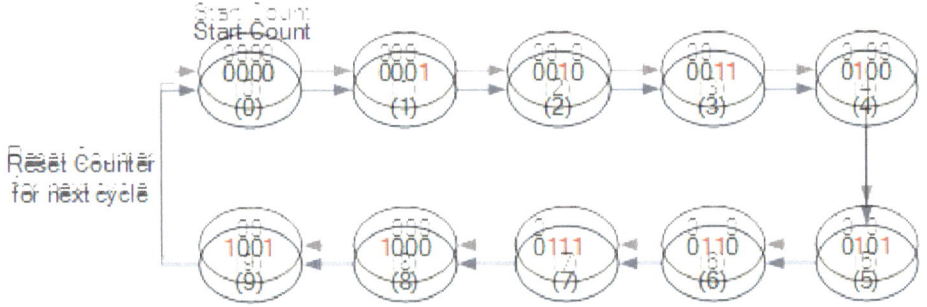

LOGIC DIAGRAM :-

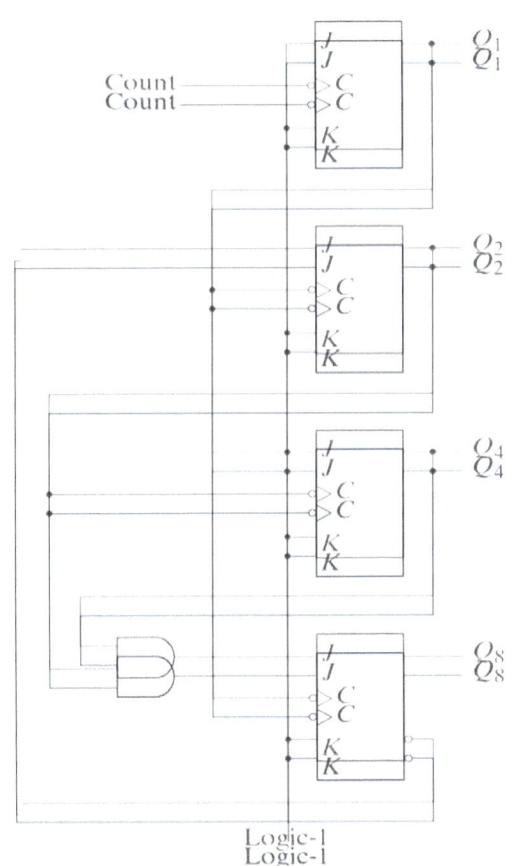

Fig. 6-10 BCD Ripple Counter

CHAPTER 2 : EXPERIMENTS PERFORMED ON IC DIGITAL TRAINER KIT

In this chapter we perform digital logic experiments using "LOGISIM" software which replaces the need of IC digital trainer kit. Before proceeding to experiments, let us know about how to install and use the software:

UNDERSTANDING LOGISIM:-

> **INTRODCTION**

Logisim ("logic simulator") is a software program for designing combinational logic circuits. We will use Logisim in this lab to help us design complex circuits. The purpose of this section is to help you become comfortable with Logisim.

> **INSTALLING LOGISIM**

- Install **Logisim** by clicking this link:
https://drive.google.com/open?id=0B6RZSBfl8gOkQjNib1l0NGhBVEE
- Install supporting **JDK(Java Development Kit)** by clicking this link:
https://drive.google.com/open?id=1yeRo6VE99AXLhRG9B80sO9oKXYCRyV67

Download and save the files to the Desktop. After the download completes, double-click **logisim-win-2.7.1.exe** and follow the given steps to install it step by step.

> **USING LOGISIM**

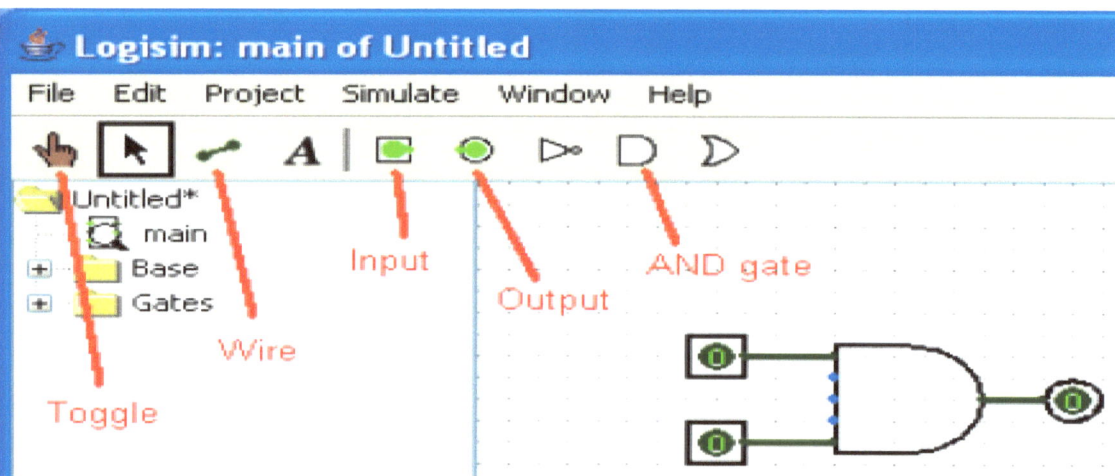

Fig(a): LOGISIM's Graphical User Interface

1. Select the **AND gate** from the toolbar (see Fig(a)), and place the gate anywhere in the dotted field.
2. Select the **Input tool**, and place two inputs to the left of the AND gate.
3. Select the **Output tool**, and place one output to the right of the AND gate.
4. Select the **Wire tool**, and draw a wire connecting the two inputs to the input pins of the AND gate. Also connect the output to the output pin of the AND gate. Your diagram should look similar to the circuit in the given figure Fig(a).
5. Use the **Toggle tool** to change the values of the inputs while observing the output. Confirm that this circuit behaves as it should.
6. To construct the Truth Table for this AND gate go to **Window -> Computational Analysis**

   In **Inputs tab** give the inputs A and B and in **Outputs tab** give Y as output. Now input the table given below in the **Table tab**. We can just input values by single or double clicks.

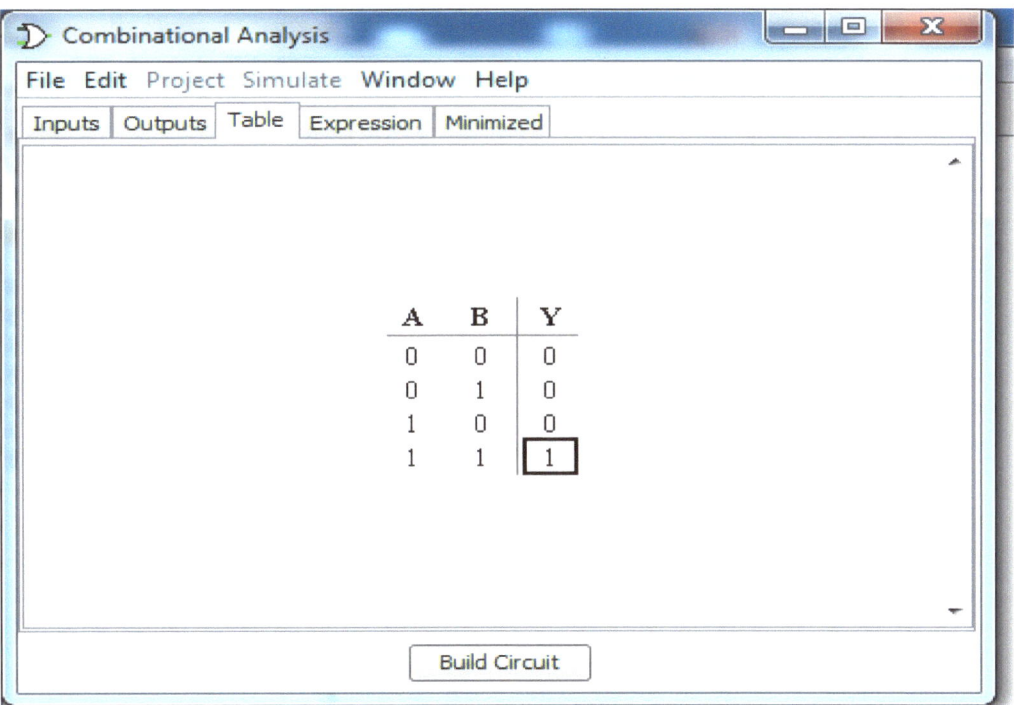

EXPERIMENTS:-

1: Realization of basic gates.

THEORY:

Logic gates are the basic building blocks of any digital system. It is an electronic circuit having one or more than one input and only one output. The relationship between the input and the output is based on a certain logic. Based on this, logic gates are named as AND gate, OR gate, NOT gate etc. Below are the symbols, boolean expression and truth table of these 3 basic gates:

1) AND gate:-

This gate gives high output (1) if all the inputs are 1's. Otherwise the output will be low (0). Its Boolean algebra representation is: C=A.B. And it's truth table and symbol as following:

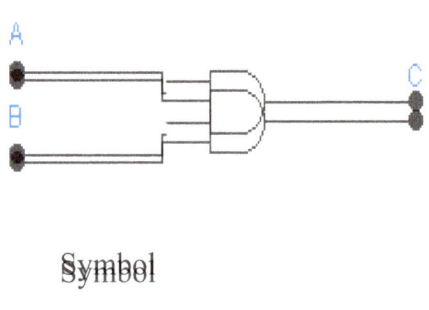

Symbol

INPUTS		OUTPUT
A	B	C
0	0	0
0	1	0
1	0	0
1	1	1

Truth table

2) OR gate:-

This circuit will give high output (1) if any input is high (1). Its Boolean algebra representation is: C=A+B. And it's truth table and schema as following:

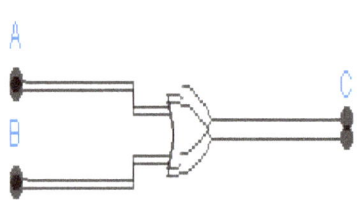

Symbol

INPUTS		OUTPUT
A	B	C
0	0	0
0	1	1
1	0	1
1	1	1

Truth table

3) NOT gate:-

This is the simplest gate which just inverts the input, if the input is high the output will be low and conversely. So its Boolean algebra representation is: B=A'. And it's truth table and schema as following:

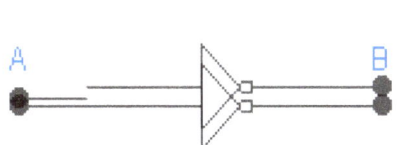

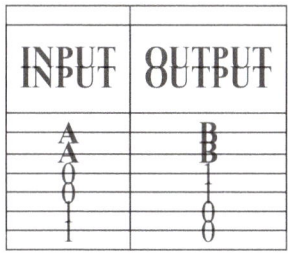

Symbol   Truth table

LOGISIM SIMULATION:

Step 1: Draw the logic diagram for each given gate using the gates from **Gates section** and connect the inputs and output as mentioned.

Step 2: Now use the **Toggle tool** to change the values of the inputs while observing the output. Confirm that this circuit behaves as it should as given in the Truth table.

REALIZATION OF DIGITAL LOGIC CIRCUIT HAVING BASIC GATES:

This can be done in two ways:

1) To realize a given digital logic circuit by finding the Boolean expression that represents the circuit.

2) To realize a given digital logic circuit by finding the truth table that represents the circuit.

Example:-

1) Realize the following digital logic circuit by finding the Boolean expression and Truth table that represent the circuit.

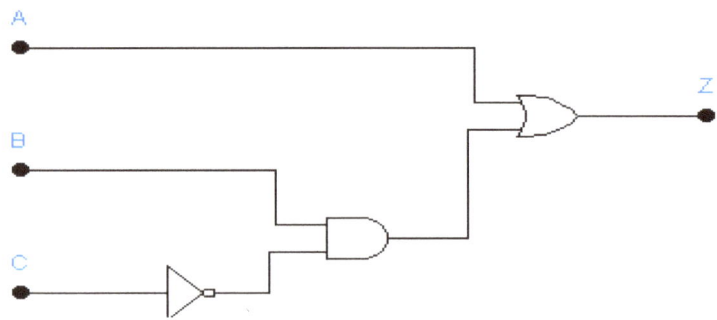

Answer:-

First the output of each gate is taken to give it as input to next gate in the circuit. Repeat this till the last gate to get the final output. The below logic circuit shows this:

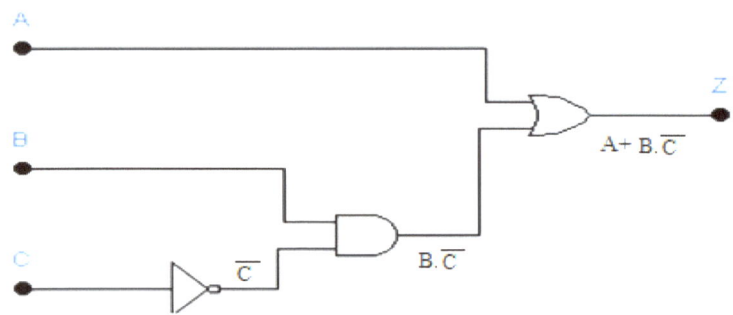

Therefore the final output is Z = A + B . C'
Similarly by seeing the gates behavior we can draw the following truth table for the above given circuit.

A	B	C	Z
0	0	0	0
0	0	1	0
0	1	0	1
0	1	1	0
1	0	0	1
1	0	1	1
1	1	0	1
1	1	1	1

Truth table

2. Realization of universal gates.

THEORY:

NAND and NOR gates are called as Universal Gates as they can be used to create all other logic gates like basic gates AND, OR, NOT and XOR, XNOR etc. That is why these two gates are the digital building blocks. Below are the symbols, boolean expression and truth table of all these gates:

Name	Symbol	Function	Truth Table
AND	A, B → X	$X = A \cdot B$ or $X = AB$	A B X 0 0 0 0 1 0 1 0 0 1 1 1
OR	A, B → X	$X = A + B$	A B X 0 0 0 0 1 1 1 0 1 1 1 1
NOT	A → X	$X = A'$	A X 0 1 1 0
NAND	A, B → X	$X = (AB)'$	A B X 0 0 1 0 1 1 1 0 1 1 1 0
NOR	A, B → X	$X = (A + B)'$	A B X 0 0 1 0 1 0 1 0 0 1 1 0
XOR (Exclusive OR)	A, B → X	$X = A \oplus B$ or $X = A'B + AB'$	A B X 0 0 0 0 1 1 1 0 1 1 1 0
XNOR (Exclusive NOR or Equivalence)	A, B → X	$X = (A \oplus B)'$ or $X = A'B' + AB$	A B X 0 0 1 0 1 0 1 0 0 1 1 1

(1) **Realization of NOT, OR, AND, XOR, XNOR gates using universal gate NAND :**

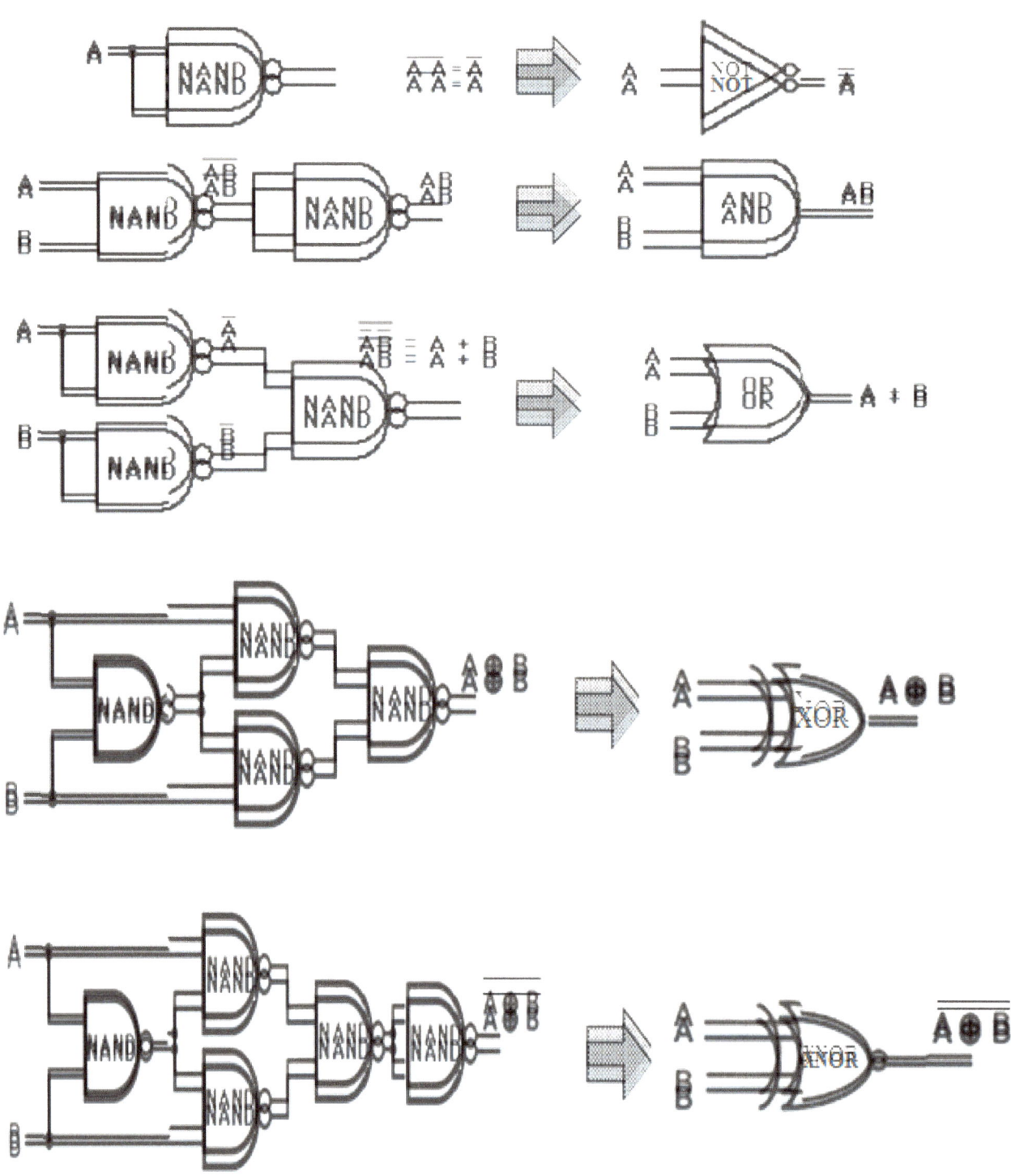

(2) **Realization of NOT, OR, AND, XOR, XNOR gates using universal gate NOR.**

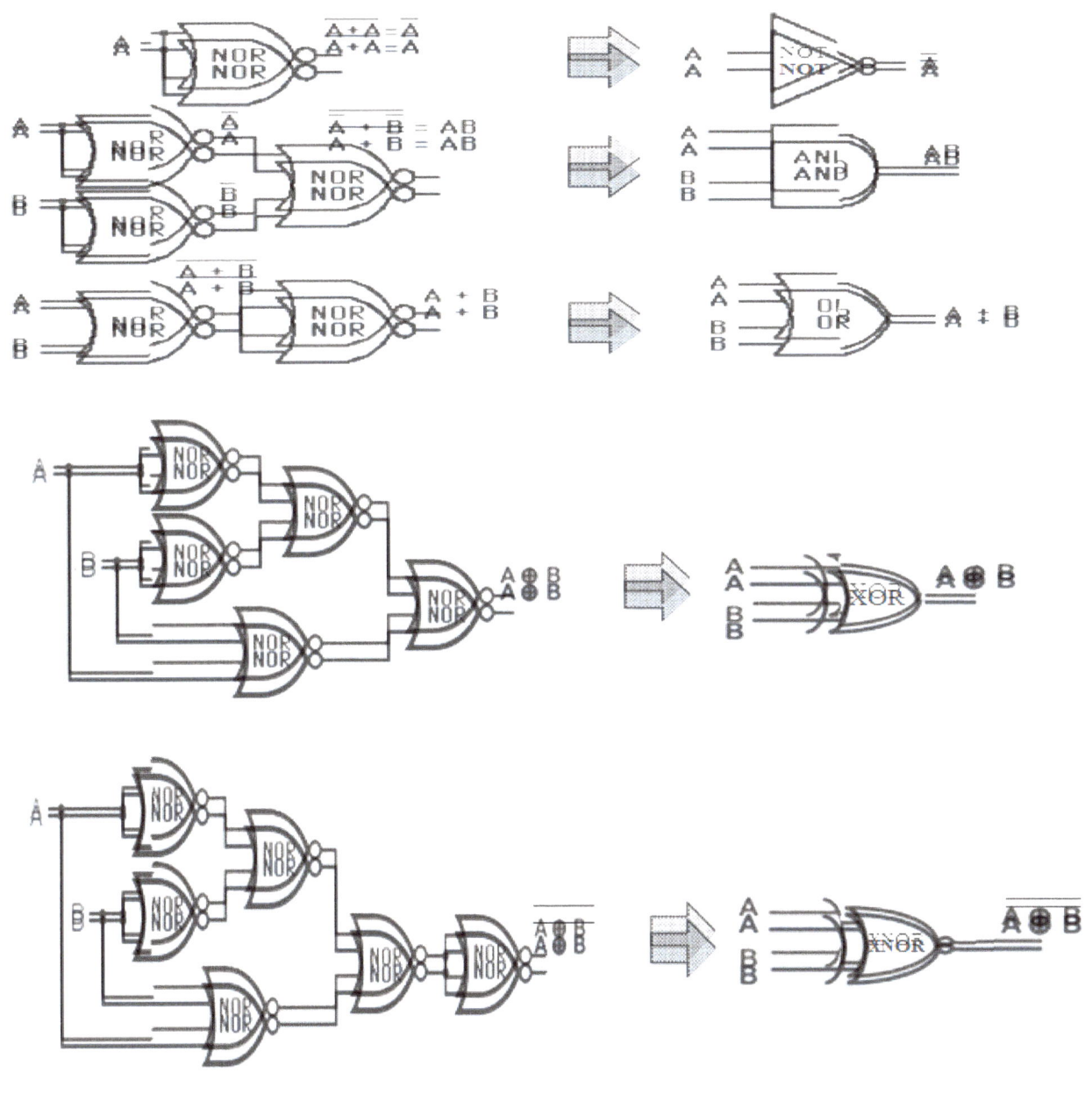

LOGISIM SIMULATION:

Step 1: Draw the logic circuit diagram as given above using the gates from **Gates section** and connect the inputs and output as mentioned.

Step 2: Now use the **Toggle tool** to change the values of the inputs while observing the output. Confirm that this circuit behaves as it should as given in the Truth table.

3. Realization of SOP expression using universal gates.

THEORY:

Sum of Product (SOP) Form

The sum-of-products (SOP) form is a method (or form) of simplifying the Boolean expressions of logic gates. In this SOP form of Boolean function representation, the variables are operated by AND (product) to form a product term and all these product terms are ORed (summed or added) together to get the final function.

Examples:-
F = AB + BC + AC.

F= AB + ABC + CDE

F = A'BC + AB'C + ABC ' + ABC

SOP form can be obtained by

- Writing an AND term for each input combination, which produces HIGH output.
- Writing the input variables if the value is 1, and write the complement of the variable if its value is 0.
- OR the AND terms to obtain the output function.

Example: Implementing the SOP expression F = A'BC + AB'C + ABC ' + ABC using NAND gates.

Simplify the given expression as follows:

By Idempotence law, we know that
([ABC + ABC] + ABC) = (ABC + ABC) = ABC

Now the function F = A'BC + AB'C + ABC ' + ABC

F= A'BC + AB'C + ABC' + ([ABC + ABC)] + ABC)

F= (ABC + ABC ') + (ABC + AB'C) + (ABC + A'BC)

F= AB (C + C ') + A (B + B') C + (A + A') BC

F= AB + BC + AC.

TRUTH TABLE:

A	B	C	F
0	0	0	0
0	0	1	0
0	1	0	0
0	1	1	1
1	0	0	0
1	0	1	1
1	1	0	1
1	1	1	1

Now write the input variables combination with high output. F = AB + BC + AC.

LOGIC DIAGRAM :

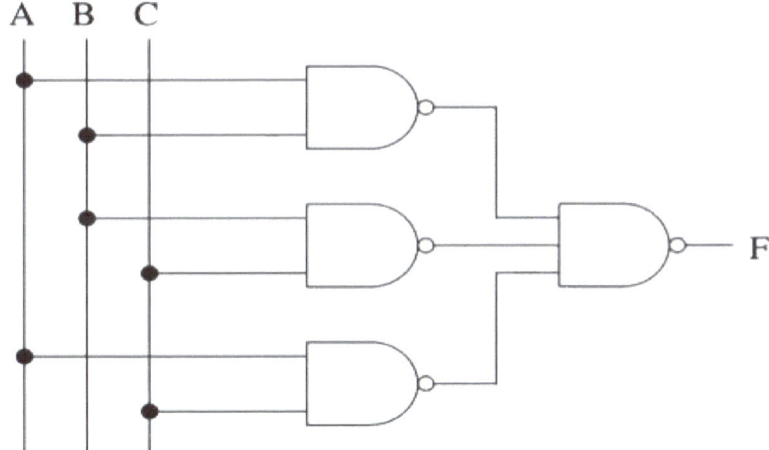

LOGISIM SIMULATION:

Step 1: Draw the logic diagram as given above using the gates from **Gates section** and connect the inputs and output as mentioned.

Step 2: Now use the **Toggle tool** to change the values of the inputs while observing the output. Confirm that this circuit behaves as it should as given in the Truth table.

4 : Realization of POS expression using universal gates.

THEORY:

Product of Sums (POS) Form

The product of sums form is a method (or form) of simplifying the Boolean expressions of logic gates. In this POS form, all the variables are ORed, i.e. written as sums to form sum terms. All these sum terms are ANDed (multiplied) together to get the product-of-sum form. This form is exactly opposite to the SOP form. So this can also be said as "Dual of SOP form".

Examples:-
$F \equiv (A+B) (A + B + C) (C + D)$
$F \equiv (A + B + C)(A + B + C')(A + B' + C)(A' + B + C)$

POS form can be obtained by

- Writing an OR term for each input combination, which produces LOW output.
- Writing the input variables if the value is 0, and write the complement of the variable if its value is 1.
- AND the OR terms to obtain the output function.

Example: Implementing the POS expression $F = (A + B + C)(A + B + C')(A + B' + C)(A' + B + C)$ using NOR gates.

Simplify the given expression as follows:

By Idempotence law, we know that

$[(A + B + C) (A + B + C)] (A + B + C) = [(A + B + C)] (A + B + C) = (A + B + C)$

Now the function $F = (A + B)(B + C)(A + C)$
$\equiv (A + B + C)(A + B + C')(A + B' + C)(A' + B + C)$
$\equiv [(A + B + C)(A + B + C')](A + B + C)(A + B' + C)(A + B + C)(A' + B + C)$
$\equiv [(A + B + C)(A + B + C')][(A + B + C)(A' + B + C)][(A + B + C)(A + B' + C)]$
$\equiv [(A + B) + (C * C')][(B + C) + (A * A')][(A + C) + (B * B')]$
$\equiv [(A + B) + 0][(B + C) + 0][(A + C) + 0]$
$F \equiv (A + B)(B + C)(A + C)$

TRUTH TABLE:

A	B	C	F
0	0	0	0
0	0	1	0
0	1	0	0
0	1	1	1
1	0	0	0
1	0	1	1
1	1	0	1
1	1	1	1

Now write the input variables combination with high output. $F = (A + B)(B + C)(A + C)$

LOGIC DIAGRAM:

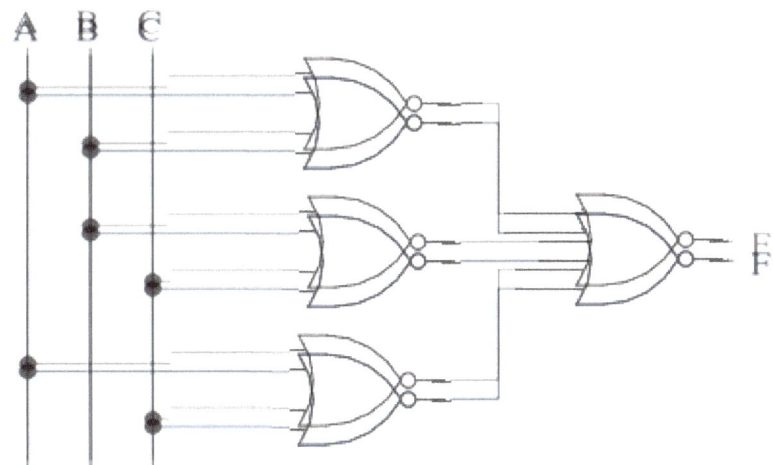

LOGISIM SIMULATION:

Step 1: Draw the logic diagram as given above using the gates from **Gates section** and connect the inputs and output as mentioned.

Step 2: Now use the **Toggle tool** to change the values of the inputs while observing the output. Confirm that this circuit behaves as it should as given in the Truth table.

5. Design half and full adder using NAND gate.

THEORY:

Half-Adder:
A combinational logic circuit that performs the addition of two data bits, A and B, is called a half-adder. Addition will result in two output bits; one of which is the sum bit, S, and the other is the carry bit, C.

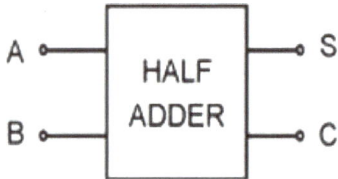

Full-Adder:

The half-adder does not take the carry bit from its previous stage into account. This carry bit from its previous stage is called carry-in bit. A combinational logic circuit that adds two data bits, A and B, and a carry-in bit, C_{in}, is called a full-adder.

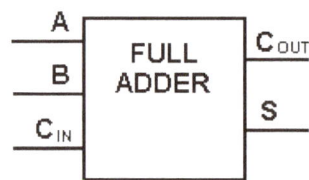

(1) Designing HALF ADDER:-

TRUTH TABLE:

INPUTS		OUTPUTS	
A	B	S	C
0	0	0	0
0	1	1	0
1	0	1	0
1	1	0	1

KARNAUGH MAPS:

For Carry   For Sum

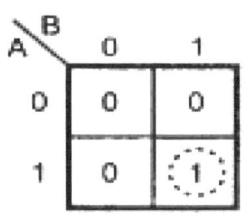 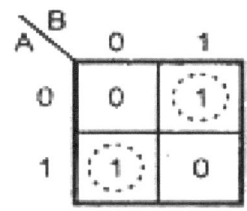

Carry = AB   Sum = $A\bar{B} + \bar{A}B$
                                           = $A \oplus B$

LOGIC DIAGRAM:

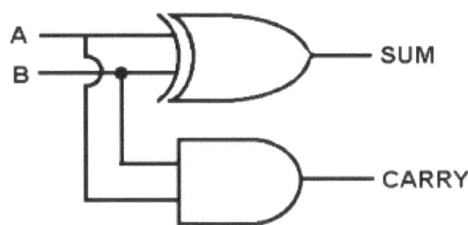

(a) Circuit Diagram Of Half Adder

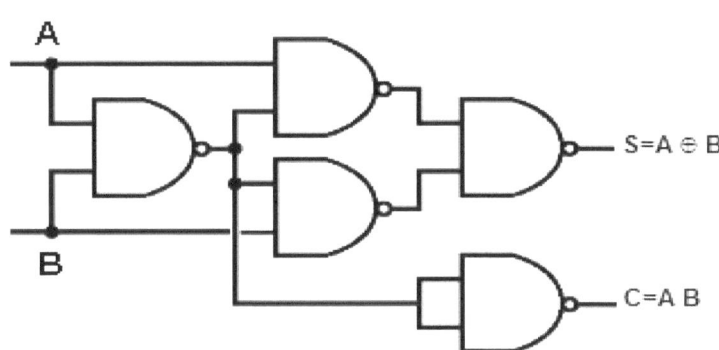

(b) Half adder Circuit Diagram using NAND gates.

(2) Designing FULL ADDER:-

TRUTH TABLE:

INPUTS			OUTPUTS	
A	B	C_{in}	S	C
0	0	0	0	0
0	0	1	1	0
0	1	0	1	0
0	1	1	0	1
1	0	0	1	0
1	0	1	0	1
1	1	0	0	1
1	1	1	1	1

KARNAUGH MAPS:

For Carry (C_{out})   For Sum

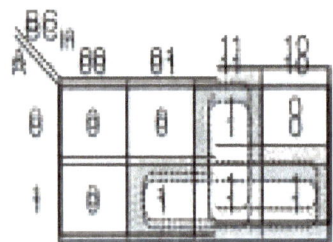 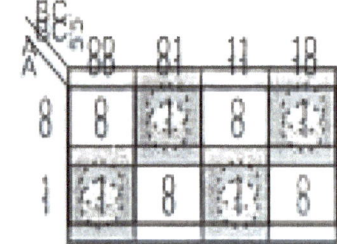

$C_{out} = AB + AC_{in} + BC_{in}$

$Sum = \bar{A}\bar{B}C_{in} + \bar{A}B\bar{C}_{in} + A\bar{B}\bar{C}_{in} + ABC_{in}$

$$Sum = \bar{A}\bar{B}C_{in} + \bar{A}B\bar{C}_{in} + A\bar{B}\bar{C}_{in} + ABC_{in}$$
$$= C_{in}(\bar{A}\bar{B} + AB) + \bar{C}_{in}(\bar{A}B + A\bar{B})$$
$$= C_{in}(A \odot B) + \bar{C}_{in}(A \oplus B)$$
$$= C_{in}(\overline{A \oplus B}) + \bar{C}_{in}(A \oplus B)$$
$$= C_{in} \oplus (A \oplus B)$$

i.e., $Sum = A \oplus B \oplus C_{in}$

LOGIC DIAGRAM:

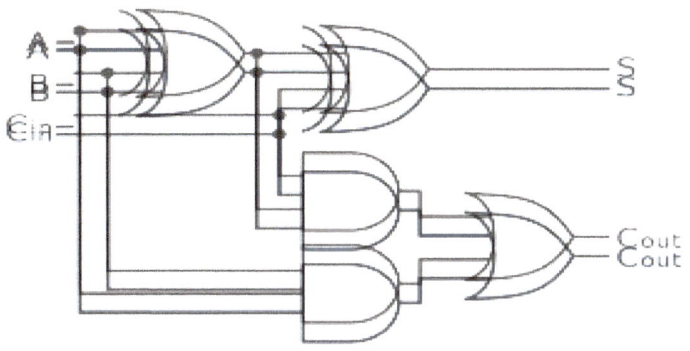

(a) Circuit Diagram Of Full Adder

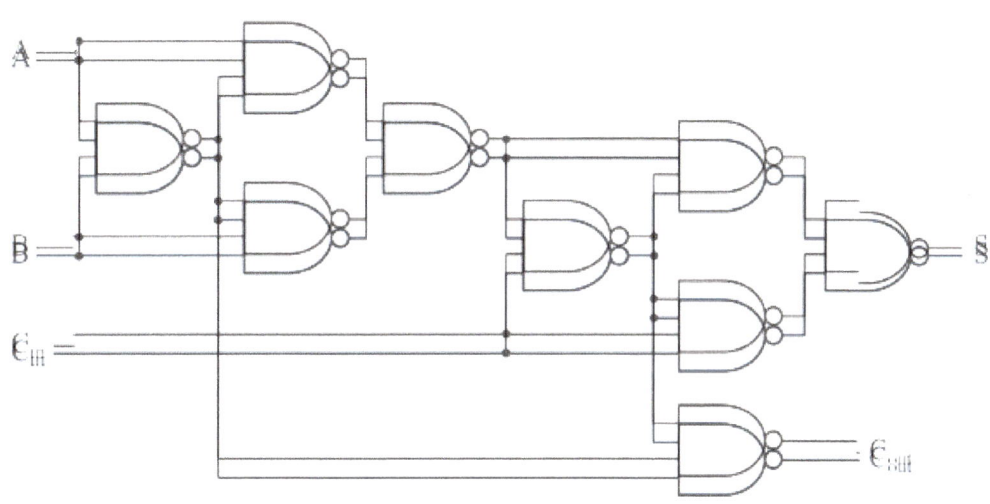

(b) Full adder Circuit Diagram using NAND gates.

LOGISIM SIMULATION:

Step 1: Draw the logic diagram as given above for half and full adders using the NAND gates from **Gates section** and connect the inputs and output as mentioned.

Step 2: Now use the **Toggle tool** to change the values of the inputs while observing the output. Confirm that this circuit behaves as it should as given in the Truth table.

6. Design half and full subtractor using NAND gate.

THEORY:

Half Subtractor:

Subtracting a single-bit binary value B from another A (i.e. A -B) produces a difference bit D and a borrow out bit Bo. This operation is called half subtraction and the circuit to realize it is called a half subtractor.

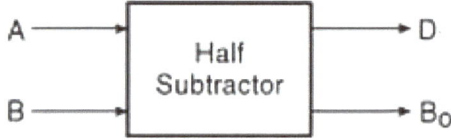

Full Subtractor:

Subtracting two single-bit binary values, B, C_{in} from a single-bit value A (i.e., A-(B and B_{in}))produces a difference bit D and a borrow out B_{Out} bit. This is called full subtraction.

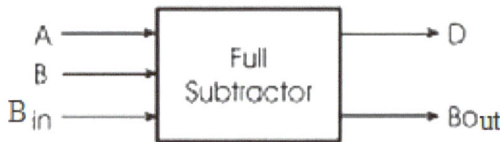

(1) Designing HALF SUBTRACTOR:-

TRUTH TABLE:

Input		Output	
A	B	Difference	Borrow
0	0	0	0
0	1	1	1
1	0	1	0
1	1	0	0

KARNAUGH MAPS:

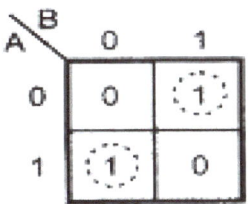

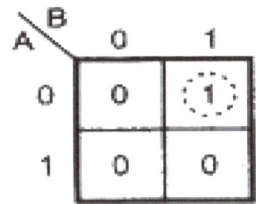

Difference = $A\bar{B} + \bar{A}B$
= $A \oplus B$

Borrow = $\bar{A}B$

LOGIC DIAGRAM:

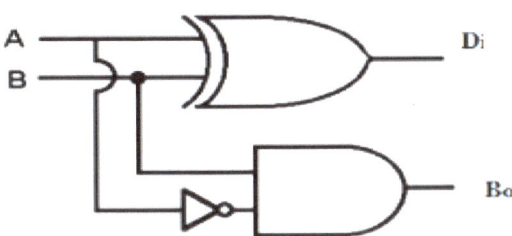

(a) **Circuit Diagram Of Half Subtractor**

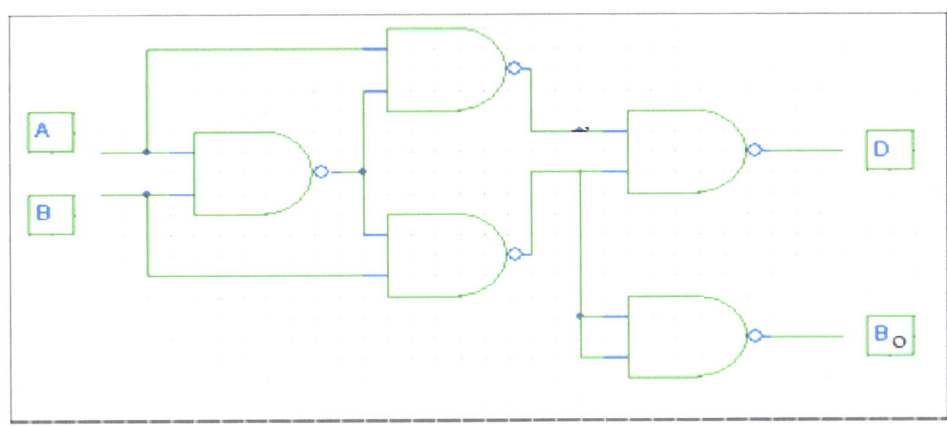

(b) **Half Subtractor Circuit Diagram using NAND gates.**

(2) Designing FULL SUBTRACTOR:-

TRUTH TABLE:-

A	B	B_{in}	D	B_{out}
0	0	0	0	0
0	0	1	1	1
0	1	0	1	1
0	1	1	0	0
1	0	0	1	0
1	0	1	0	0
1	1	0	0	0
1	1	1	1	1

KARNAUGH MAPS:

For D

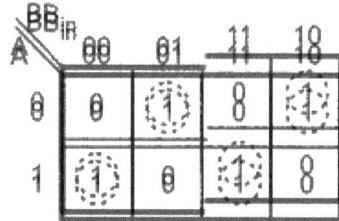

For B_{out}

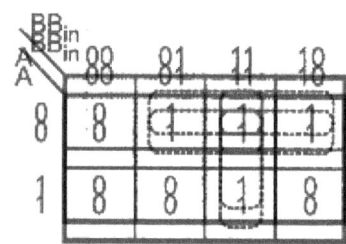

$D = \overline{A}\overline{B}B_{in} + \overline{A}B\overline{B_{in}} + A\overline{B}\overline{B_{in}} + ABB_{in}$

$B_{out} = \overline{A}B_{in} + \overline{A}B + BB_{in}$

$D \equiv \overline{A}\,\overline{B}\,B_{in} + \overline{A}\,B\,\overline{B_{in}} + A\,\overline{B}\,\overline{B_{in}} + A\,B\,B_{in}$

$\quad = B_{in}(\overline{A}\,\overline{B} + AB) + \overline{B_{in}}(\overline{A}B + A\overline{B})$

$\quad = B_{in}(A \odot B) + \overline{B_{in}}(A \oplus B)$

$\quad = B_{in}(\overline{A \oplus B}) + \overline{B_{in}}(A \oplus B)$

$\quad = B_{in} \oplus (A \oplus B)$

i.e., $D \equiv A \oplus B \oplus B_{in}$

LOGIC DIAGRAM:

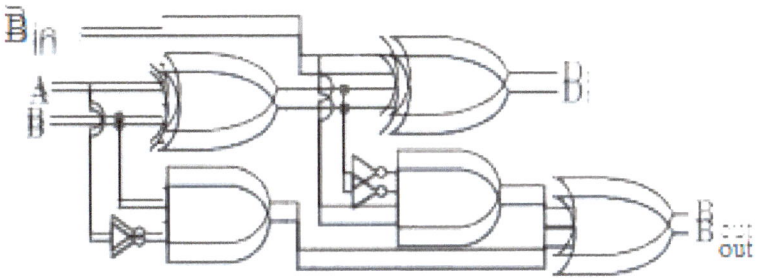

(a) Circuit Diagram Of Full Subtractor

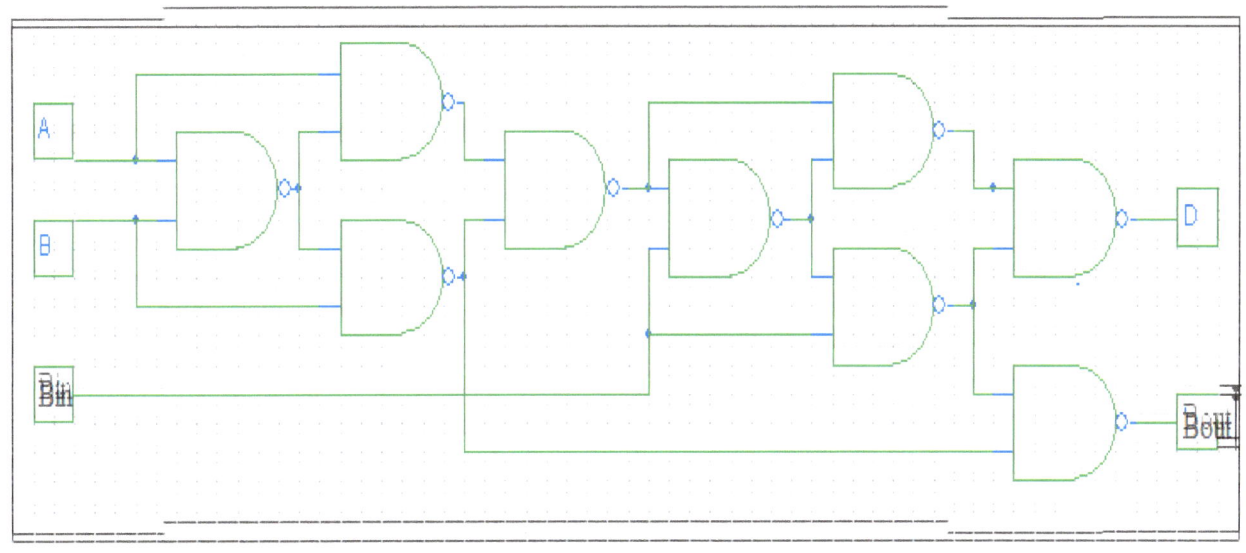

(b) Full Subtractor Circuit Diagram using NAND gates:

LOGISIM SIMULATION:

Step 1: Draw the logic diagram as given above for half and full subtractor using the NAND gates from **Gates section** and connect the inputs and output as mentioned.

Step 2: Now use the **Toggle tool** to change the values of the inputs while observing the output. Confirm that this circuit behaves as it should as given in the Truth table.

7. Realization of parallel adder/ subtractor using IC and XOR gate.

THEORY:

Parallel Adder / Subtractor:-
The operations of both addition and subtraction can be performed by a one common binary adder. Such binary circuit can be designed by adding an Ex-OR gate with each **full adder** as shown in below figure. The figure below shows the **4 bit parallel binary adder/subtractor** which has two 4 bit inputs as A3 A2 A1 A0 and B3 B2 B1 B0.

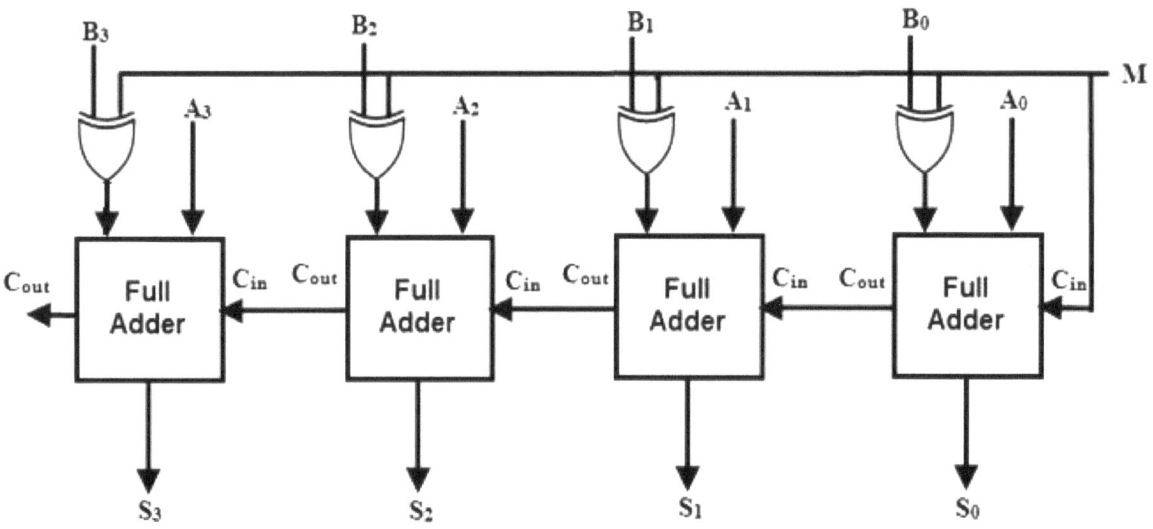

Logic diagram of 4 bit parallel binary adder/subtractor

The **mode input control line M** is connected with **carry input** of the least significant bit of the full adder. **This control line decides the type of operation, whether addition or subtraction.** When **M= 1, the circuit is a subtractor** and when **M=0, the circuit becomes adder**. The Ex-OR gate consists of two inputs to which one is connected to the B and other to input M.

When M = 0, B Ex-OR of 0 produce B. Then full adders add the B with A with carry input zero and hence an addition operation is performed.

Example 1:- 7+2=11 (1001)
7 is realized at A3 A2 A1 A0 = 0111
2 is realized at B3 B2 B1 B0 = 0010
                    Sum = 1001

When M = 1, B Ex-OR of 0 produce B complement and also carry input is 1. Hence the complemented B inputs are added to A and 1 is added through the input carry, nothing but a 2's complement operation. Therefore, the subtraction operation is performed.

Example 2:- 8 – 3 = 5 (0101)

8 is realized at A3 A2 A1 A0 = 1000
3 is realized at B3 B2 B1 B0 through X-OR gates = 0011
• Output of X-OR gate is 1's complement of 3 = 1100
• 2's Complement can be obtained by adding Cin = 1

Therefore
Cin = 1
A3 A2 A1 A0 = 1 0 0 0
B3 B2 B1 B0 = 1 1 0 0
S3 S2 S1 S0 =   0 1 0 1
Cout = 1 (Ignored)

LOGISIM SIMULATION:

1) **Following snapshot shows the simulation output part for the above given example (1).**

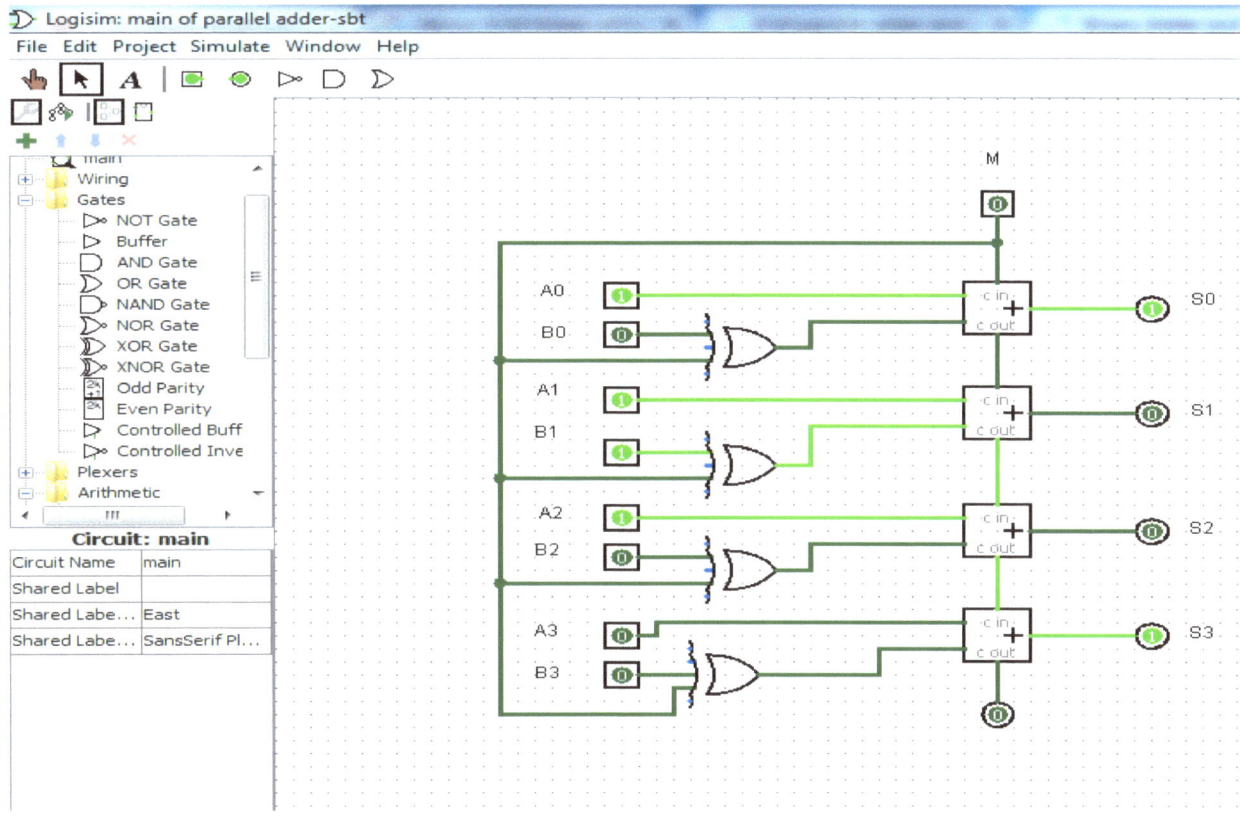

2) Following snapshot shows the simulation output part for the above given example (2):

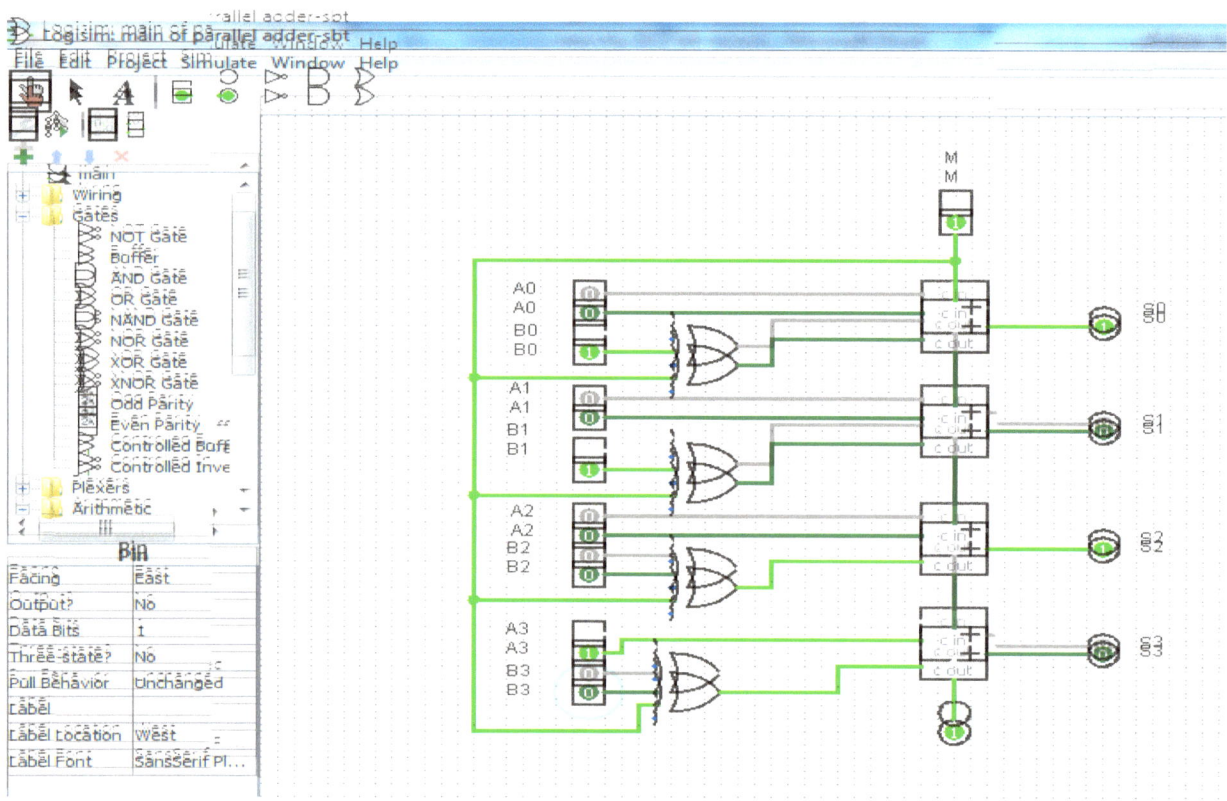

Design Steps:

1) Draw 4 binary adders by selecting Arithmetic->Adder circuit which looks like

Where, the pins mean as given in the following diagram:

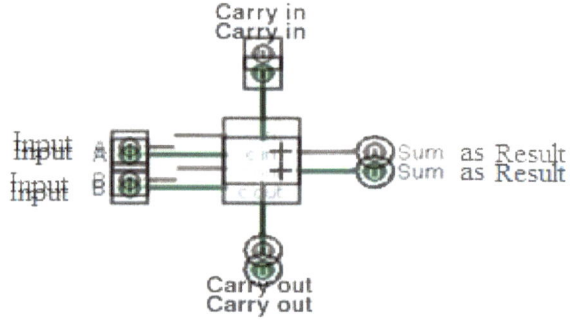

And set Adder circuit's, inputs' and outputs' **Data Bits** property as 1 since we need 1 bit binary adder.

2) Next complete the whole logic circuit connections as given in the above diagram.

3) Use the Toggle tool to change the values of the A3-A0 and B3-B0 observing the output S3-S0. Confirm that this circuit behaves as it should as given in the example(1) and (2).

8: Realization of code conversion from BCD to Ex-3 and vice versa.

THEORY:

> **BCD to Ex-3 code conversion:-**

Steps given below show how to do this type of conversion.

1) Convert BCD to decimal.
2) Add $(3)_{10}$ to this decimal number.
3) Convert into binary to get excess-3 code.

Example:- Convert $(1001)_{BCD}$ to Excess-3.

Step 1 = Convert to decimal

$(1001)_{BCD} \equiv 9_{10}$

Step 2 = Add 3 to decimal

$(9)_{10} + (3)_{10} \equiv (12)_{10}$

Step 3 = Convert to Excess-3

$(12)_{10} \equiv (1100)_2$

Result: $(1001)_{BCD} \equiv (1100)_{Ex-3}$

➤ Ex-3 to BCD code conversion:-

Steps given below show how to do this type of conversion.

1) Convert Ex-3 to decimal.
2) Subtract $(3)_{10}$ from this decimal number.
3) Convert into binary to get BCD code.

Example :- Convert $(1001)_{Ex-3}$ to BCD.
Step 1 − Convert to decimal

$(1001)_{BCD} = 9_{10}$

Step 2 − Subtract 3 from decimal
$(9)_{10} - (3)_{10} = (6)_{10}$

Step 3 − Convert to BCD
$(6)_{10} = (0110)_2$

Result: $(1001)_{Ex-3} = (0110)_{BCD}$

(i)   To design and implement 4-bit BCD to Excess -3 code converter

TRUTH TABLE:

BCD input				Excess − 3 output			
B3	B2	B1	B0	E3	E2	E1	E0
0	0	0	0	0	0	1	1
0	0	0	1	0	1	0	0
0	0	1	0	0	1	0	1
0	0	1	1	0	1	1	0
0	1	0	0	0	1	1	1
0	1	0	1	1	0	0	0
0	1	1	0	1	0	0	1
0	1	1	1	1	0	1	0
1	0	0	0	1	0	1	1
1	0	0	1	1	1	0	0
1	0	1	0	x	x	x	x
1	0	1	1	x	x	x	x
1	1	0	0	x	x	x	x
1	1	0	1	x	x	x	x
1	1	1	0	x	x	x	x
1	1	1	1	x	x	x	x

Note: Only 0- 9 combinations are considered because it is decimal numeral range. Therefore other combinations of inputs are put as 'x '(don't care) as outputs.

KARNAUGH MAPS:

K-Map for E3:

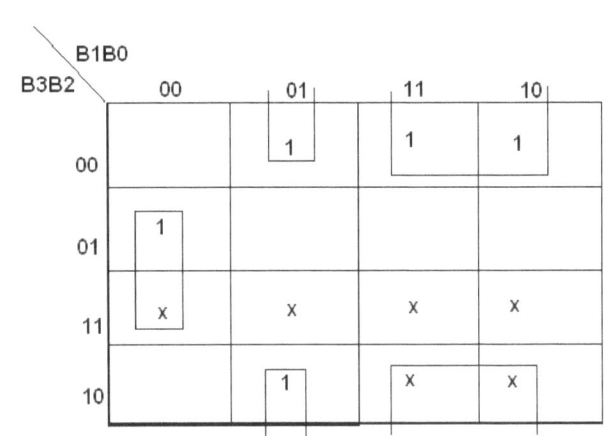

$$E3 = B3 + B2(B0 + B1)$$

K-Map for E2:

$$E2 = B2 \oplus (B1 + B0)$$

K-Map for E1:

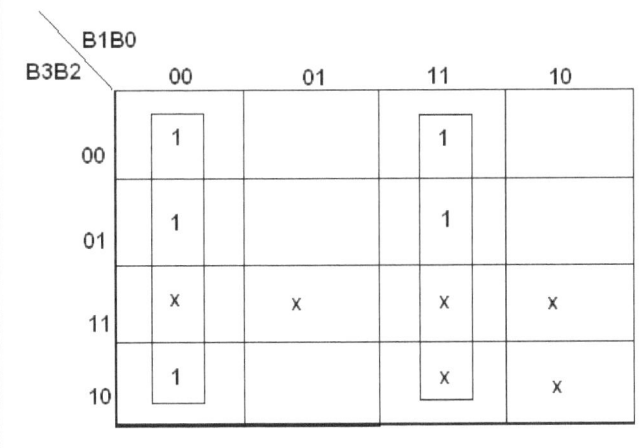

$$E1 = B1 \oplus B0$$

K-Map for E0:

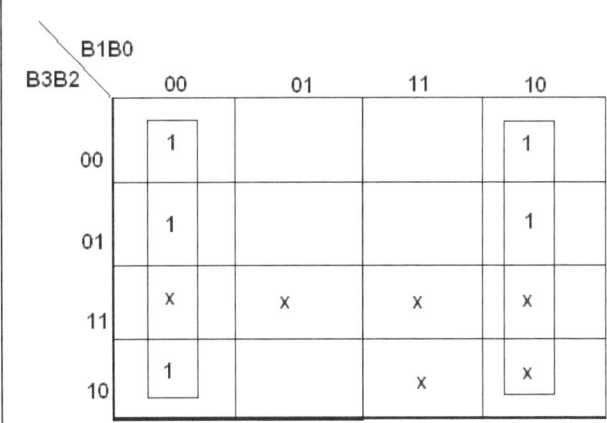

$$E0 = \overline{B0}$$

LOGIC DIAGRAM:

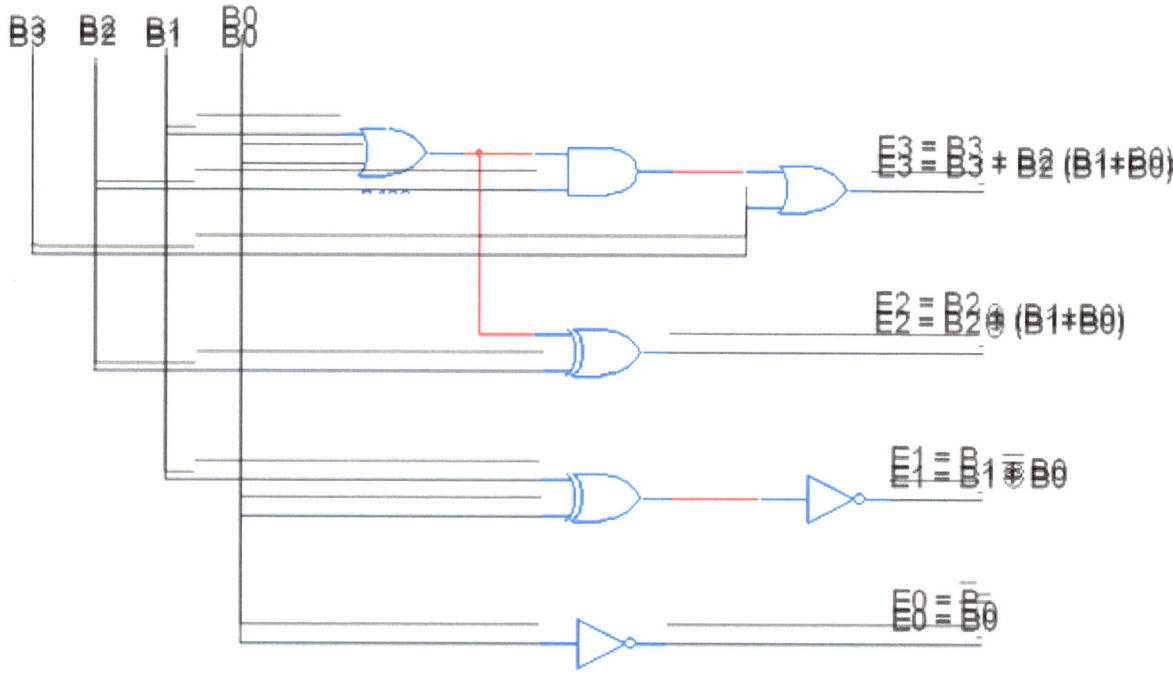

The input variables are designated as B_3, B_2, B_1, B_0 and the output variables are designated as E_3, E_2, E_1, E_0, where B_3 is most significant bit and B_0 is least significant bit.

LOGISIM SIMULATION:

Step 1: Draw the logic diagram as shown above using the gates from **Gates section** and connect the inputs and output as mentioned.

Step 2: Now use the **Toggle tool** to change the values of the inputs while observing the output. Confirm that this circuit behaves as it should as given in the Truth table.

(ii) To design and implement 4-bit Excess-3 to BCD code converter

TRUTH TABLE:

Excess – 3 Input				BCD Output			
X4	X3	X2	X1	A	B	C	D
0	0	1	1	0	0	0	0
0	1	0	0	0	0	0	1
0	1	0	1	0	0	1	0
0	1	1	0	0	0	1	1
0	1	1	1	0	1	0	0
1	0	0	0	0	1	0	1
1	0	0	1	0	1	1	0
1	0	1	0	0	1	1	1
1	0	1	1	1	0	0	0
1	1	0	0	1	0	0	1

Note: For the left out other combinations of inputs put 'x' (don't care) as outputs.

KARNAUGH MAPS:

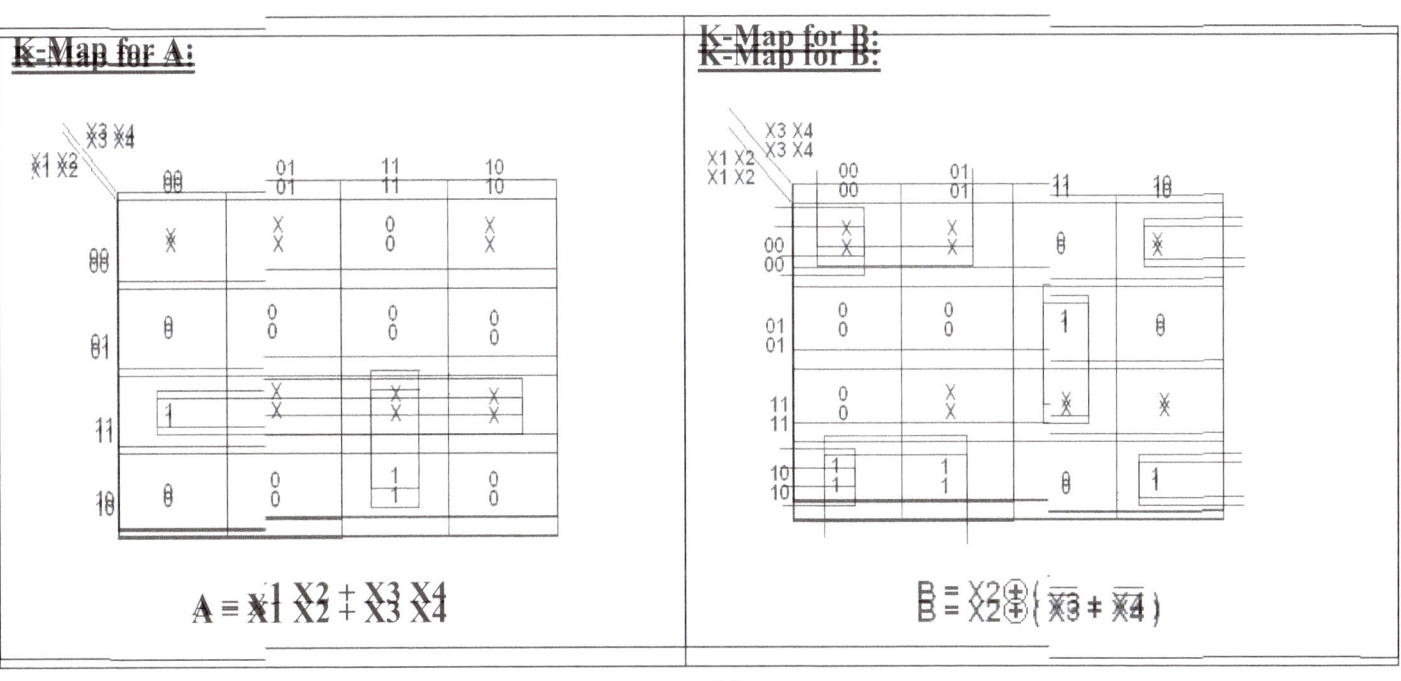

K-Map for A:

$A = X1\,X2 + X3\,X4$

K-Map for B:

$B = X2 \oplus (\overline{X3} + \overline{X4})$

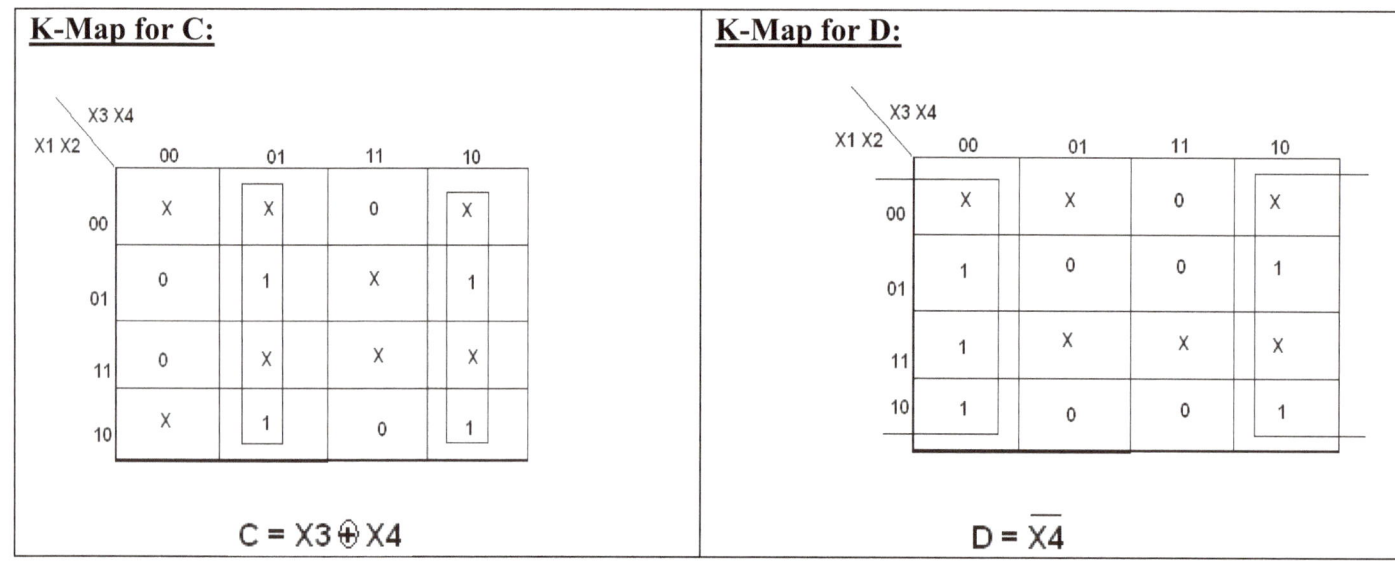

LOGIC DIAGRAM:

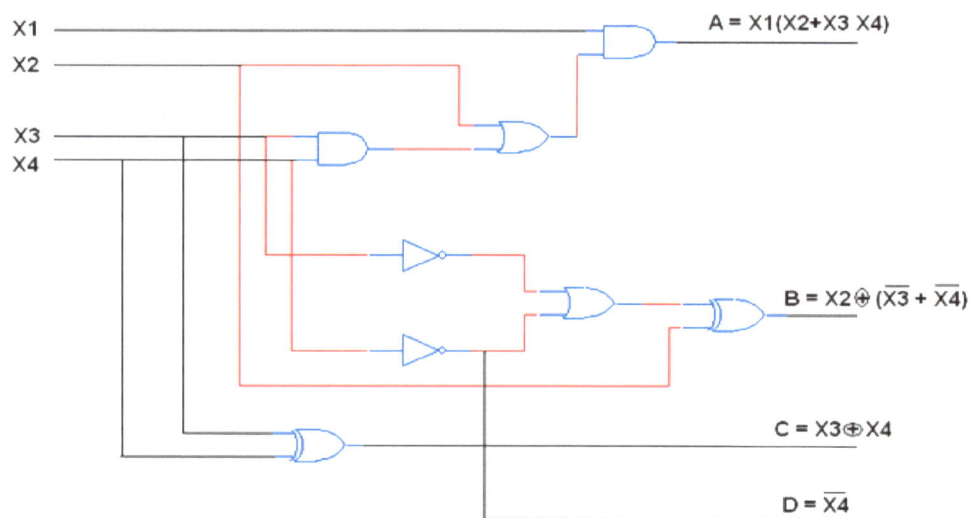

The input variable are designated as X4, X3, X2, X1 and the output variables are designated as A,B,C,D, where X4 is most significant bit and X1 is least significant bit.

LOGISIM SIMULATION:

Step 1: Draw the logic diagram as shown above using the gates from **Gates section** and connect the inputs and output as mentioned.

Step 2: Now use the **Toggle tool** 👆 to change the values of the inputs while observing the output. Confirm that this circuit behaves as it should as given in the Truth table.

9. Realization of code conversion from Gray to Binary and vice versa.

THEORY:

❖ Binary to gray code conversion:-

Steps given below show how to do this type of conversion.

1. The M.S.B. of the gray code will be exactly equal to the first bit of the given binary number.
2. Now the second bit of the code will be exclusive-or of the first and second bit of the given binary number, i.e. if both the bits are same the result will be 0 and if they are different the result will be 1.
3. The third bit of gray code will be equal to the exclusive-or of the second and third bit of the given binary number. Thus the Binary to gray code conversion goes on. One example given below explains this type of conversion.

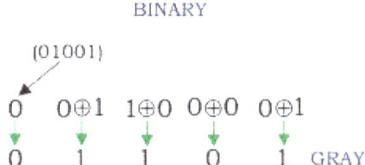

❖ Gray code to binary conversion:-

Steps given below show how to do this type of conversion.

1. The M.S.B of the binary number will be equal to the M.S.B of the given gray code.
2. Now if the second gray bit is 0 the second binary bit will be same as the previous or the first bit. If the gray bit is 1 the second binary bit will alter. If it was 1 it will be 0 and if it was 0 it will be 1.
3. This step is continued for all the bits to do Gray code to binary conversion. One example given below explains this type of conversion.

```
0   1   1   0   1   GRAY
↓   ↓   ↓   ↓   ↓
0 → 1 → 0 → 0 → 1   BINARY
```

(i) To design and implement 4-bit Binary to gray code converter

TRUTH TABLE:

Binary input				Gray code output			
B3	B2	B1	B0	G3	G2	G1	G0
0	0	0	0	0	0	0	0
0	0	0	1	0	0	0	1
0	0	1	0	0	0	1	1
0	0	1	1	0	0	1	0
0	1	0	0	0	1	1	0
0	1	0	1	0	1	1	1
0	1	1	0	0	1	0	1
0	1	1	1	0	1	0	0
1	0	0	0	1	1	0	0
1	0	0	1	1	1	0	1
1	0	1	0	1	1	1	1
1	0	1	1	1	1	1	0
1	1	0	0	1	0	1	0
1	1	0	1	1	0	1	1
1	1	1	0	1	0	0	1
1	1	1	1	1	0	0	0

KARNAUGH MAPS:

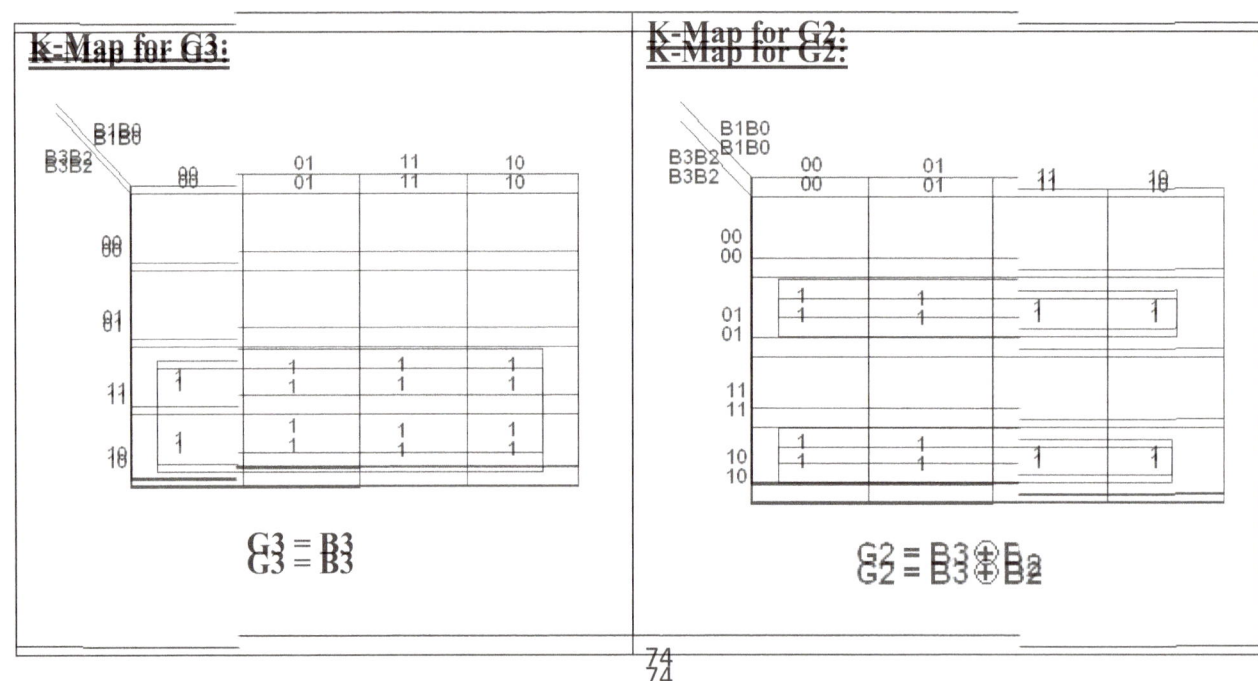

K-Map for G3:

$G3 = B3$

K-Map for G2:

$G2 = B3 \oplus B2$

K-Map for G1:

K-Map for G0:

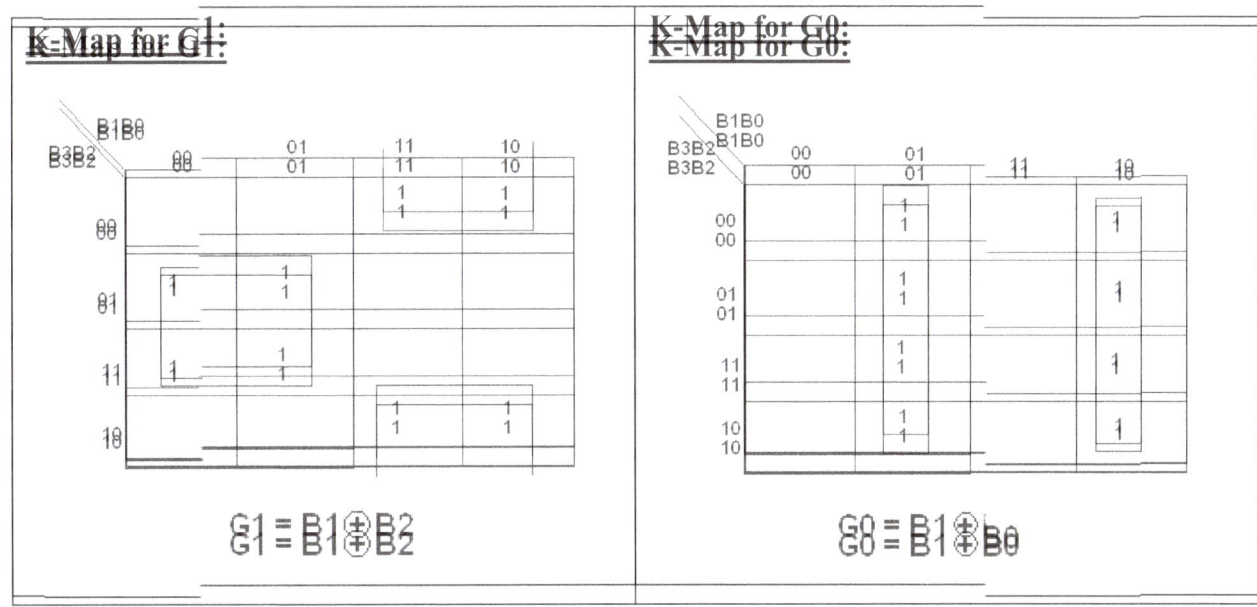

$$G1 = B1 \oplus B2$$

$$G0 = B1 \oplus B0$$

LOGIC DIAGRAM:

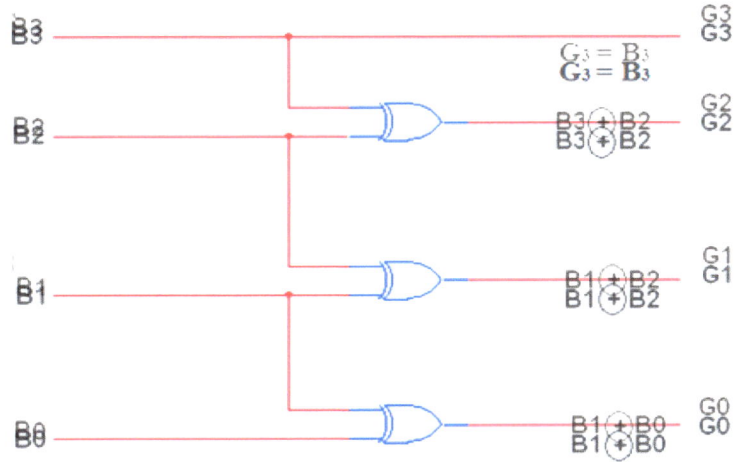

The input variable are designated as B3, B2, B1, B0 and the output variables are designated as G3, G2, G1, G0, where B_3 is most significant bit and B_0 is least significant bit.

LOGISIM SIMULATION:

Step 1: Draw the logic diagram as shown above using the gates from **Gates section** and connect the inputs and output as mentioned.

Step 2: Now use the **Toggle tool** to change the values of the inputs while observing the output. Confirm that this circuit behaves as it should as given in the Truth table.

(ii) **To design and implement 4-bit Gray to binary code converter**

TRUTH TABLE:

Gray Code				Binary Code			
G3	G2	G1	G0	B3	B2	B1	B0
0	0	0	0	0	0	0	0
0	0	0	1	0	0	0	1
0	0	1	1	0	0	1	0
0	0	1	0	0	0	1	1
0	1	1	0	0	1	0	0
0	1	1	1	0	1	0	1
0	1	0	1	0	1	1	0
0	1	0	0	0	1	1	1
1	1	0	0	1	0	0	0
1	1	0	1	1	0	0	1
1	1	1	1	1	0	1	0
1	1	1	0	1	0	1	1
1	0	1	0	1	1	0	0
1	0	1	1	1	1	0	1
1	0	0	1	1	1	1	0
1	0	0	0	1	1	1	1

KARNAUGH MAPS:

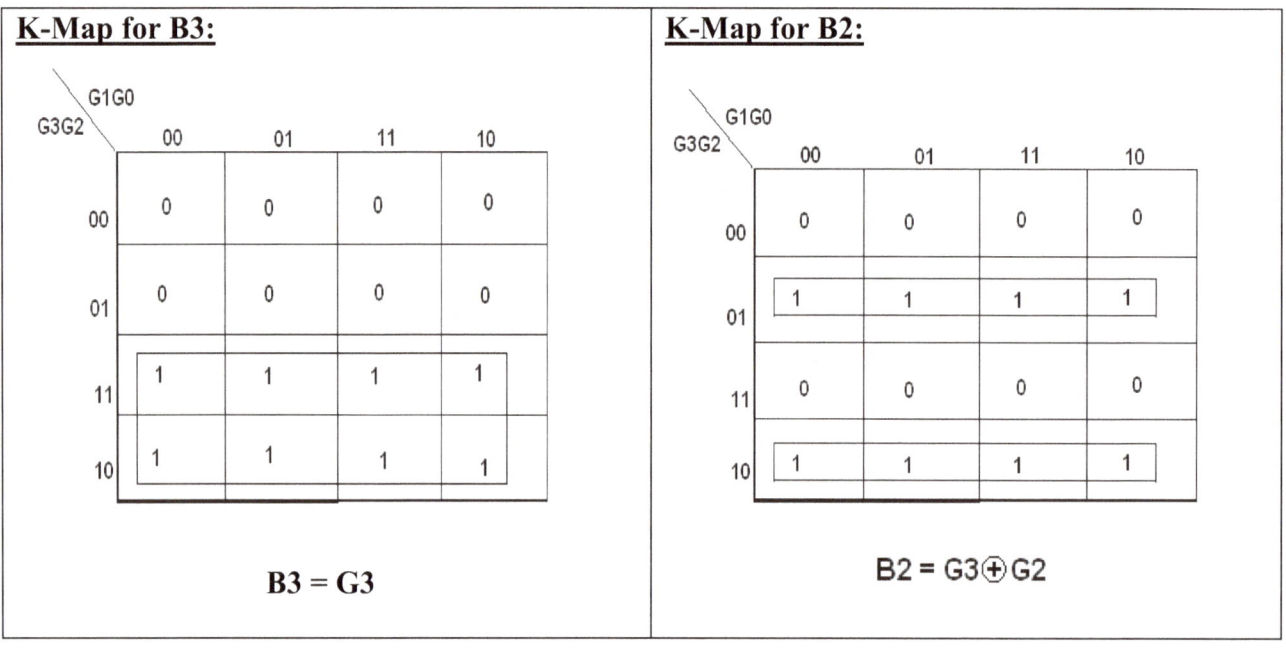

K-Map for B3:

B3 = G3

K-Map for B2:

B2 = G3 ⊕ G2

K-Map for B1:

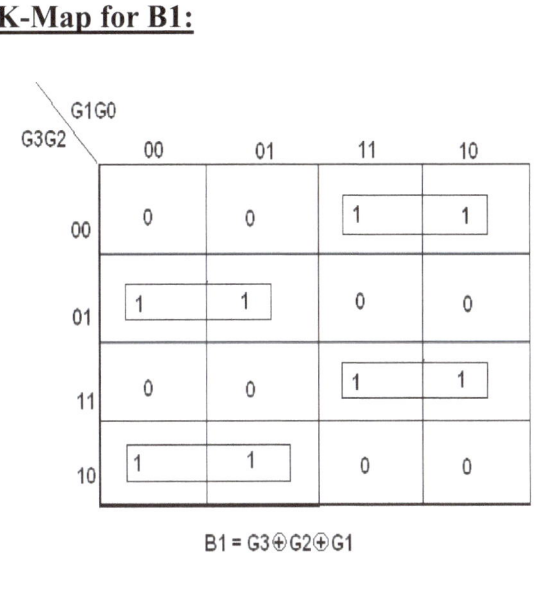

$B1 = G3 \oplus G2 \oplus G1$

K-Map for B0:

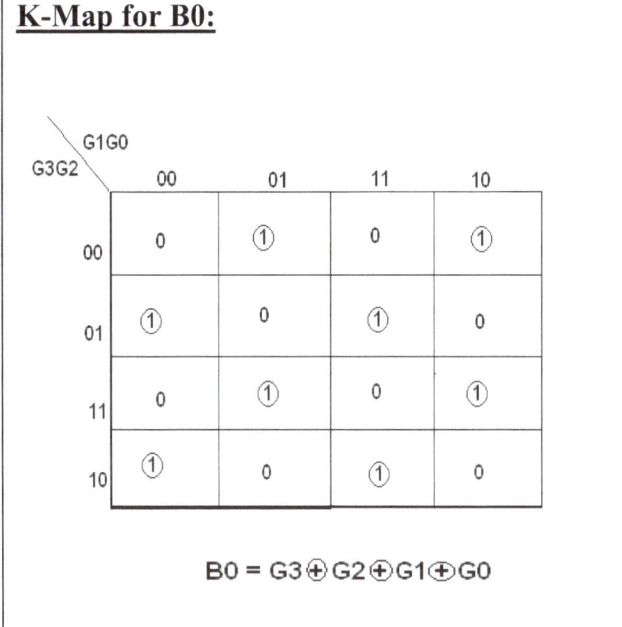

$B0 = G3 \oplus G2 \oplus G1 \oplus G0$

LOGIC DIAGRAM:

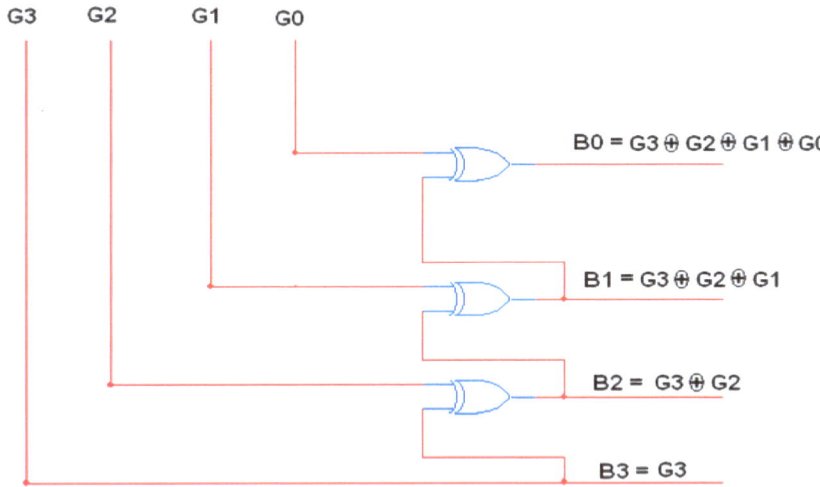

The input variable are designated as G3, G2, G1, G0 and the output variables are designated as B3, B2, B1, B0, where G3 is most significant bit and G0 is least significant bit.

LOGISIM SIMULATION:

Step 1: Draw the logic diagram as shown above using the gates from **Gates section** and connect the inputs and output as mentioned.

Step 2: Now use the **Toggle tool** to change the values of the inputs while observing the output. Confirm that this circuit behaves as it should as given in the Truth table.

10: Realization of 1-bit and 2-bit comparator using IC-7485:

THEORY:

A magnitude digital comparator is a combinational circuit that compares two digital or binary numbers (consider A and B) and determines their relative magnitudes in order to find out whether one number is equal, less than or greater than the other digital number.

Three binary variables are used to indicate the outcome of the comparison as A>B, A<B, or A=B. The below figure shows the block diagram of a n-bit comparator which compares the two numbers of n-bit length and generates their relation between themselves.

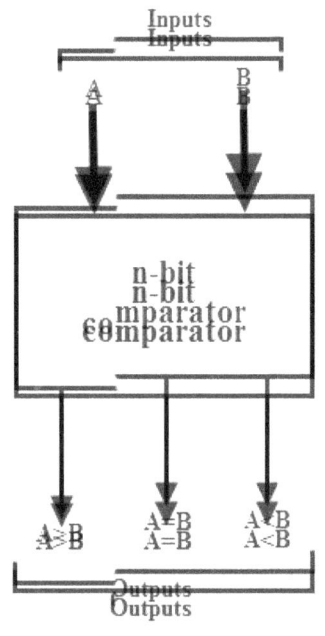

Block diagram for magnitude digital comparator

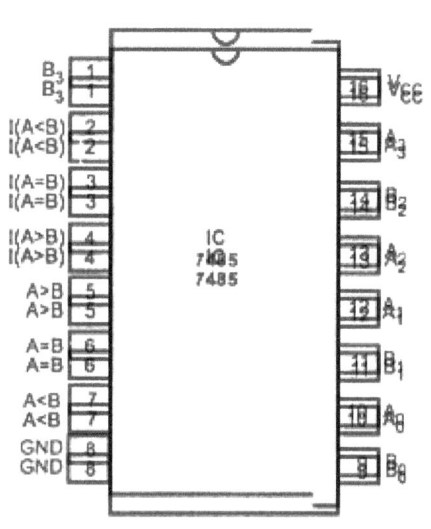

Pin diagram (IC 7485)

The IC-7485:

It is a 4-Bit Comparator which can be used to compare two four-bit words. The two 4-bit numbers are A ≡ A3 A2 A1 A0 and B3 B2 B1 B0 where A3 and B3 are the most significant bits.

One bit, two bit and four bit comparators are verified using logic gates and magnitude comparator IC7485.

1) Realization of 1-Bit comparator using logic gates :-

A comparator used to compare two bits, i.e., two numbers each of single bit is called a single bit comparator. It consists of two inputs for allowing two single bit numbers and three outputs to generate less than, equal and greater than comparison outputs.

The figure below shows the block diagram of a single bit magnitude comparator. This comparator compares the two bits and produces one of the 3 outputs as A<B, A=B and A>B.

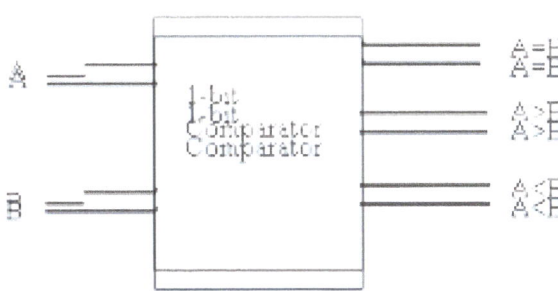

TRUTH TABLE:

INPUTS		OUTPUTS		
A	B	A>B	A=B	A<B
0	0	0	1	0
0	1	0	0	1
1	0	1	0	0
1	1	0	1	0

KARNAUGH MAPS:

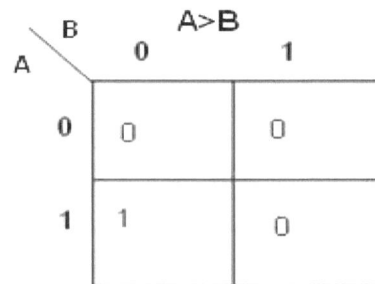

Equation is A>B = A.$\overline{B}$

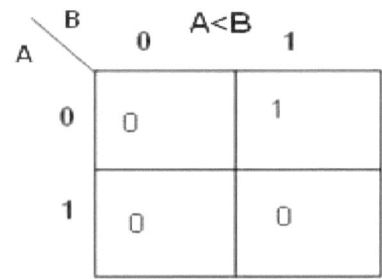

Equation is A<B = $\overline{A}$.B

A \ B	0 (A=B)	1
0	1	0
1	0	1

The equation is f(A=B) = $\overline{A}.\overline{B}$ + A.B
= A XNOR B

or we can write the equation for f(A=B) as $\overline{A.\overline{B} + \overline{A}.B}$ = $\overline{f(A>B)+f(A<B)}$

LOGIC DIAGRAM:

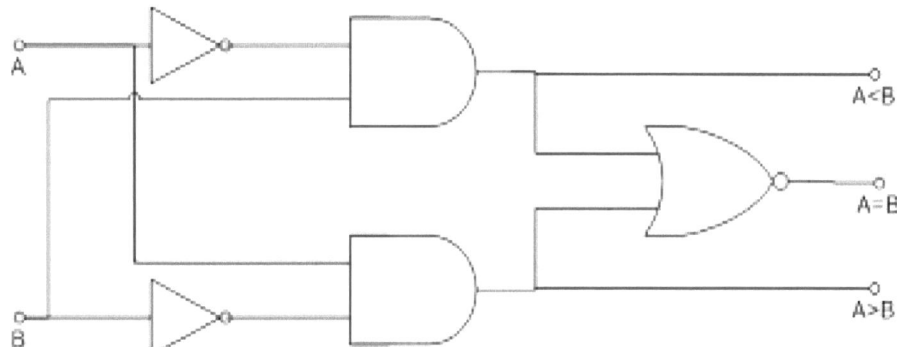

2) Realization of 2- Bit comparator using logic gates:-

A 2-bit comparator compares two binary numbers, each of two bits and produces their relation such as one number is equal or greater than or less than the other. The figure below shows the block diagram of a two-bit comparator which has four inputs and three outputs.

The first number A is designated as A = A1A0 and the second number is designated as B = B1B0. This comparator produces three outputs as A>B, A = B and A<B.

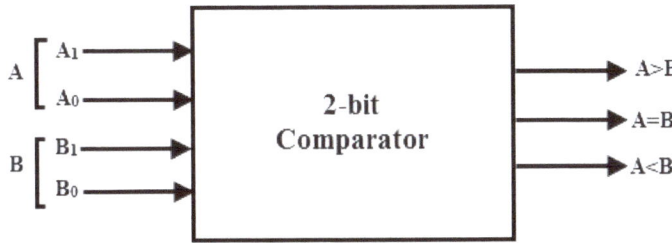

TRUTH TABLE:

INPUTS				OUTPUTS		
A_1	A_0	B_1	B_0	A > B	A = B	A < B
0	0	0	0	0	1	0
0	0	0	1	0	0	1
0	0	1	0	0	0	1
0	0	1	1	0	0	1
0	1	0	0	1	0	0
0	1	0	1	0	1	0
0	1	1	0	0	0	1
0	1	1	1	0	0	1
1	0	0	0	1	0	0
1	0	0	1	1	0	0
1	0	1	0	0	1	0
1	0	1	1	0	0	1
1	1	0	0	1	0	0
1	1	0	1	1	0	0
1	1	1	0	1	0	0
1	1	1	1	0	1	0

KARNAUGH MAPS:

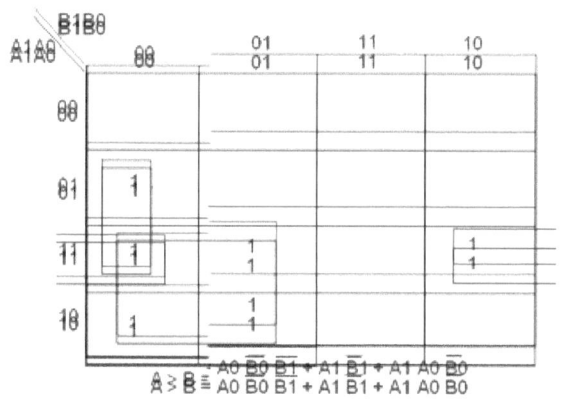

$$A > B = A0\ \overline{B0}\ \overline{B1} + A1\ \overline{B1} + A1\ A0\ \overline{B0}$$

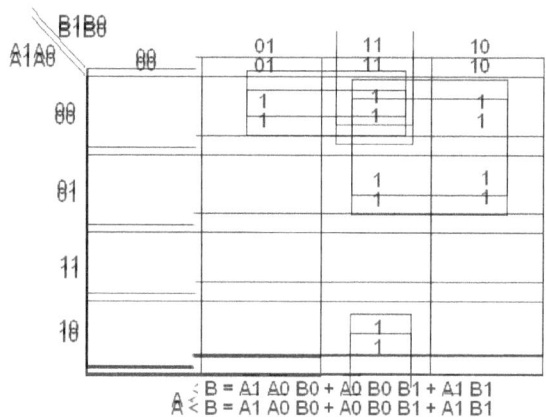

$$A < B = \overline{A1}\ \overline{A0}\ B0 + \overline{A0}\ B0\ B1 + \overline{A1}\ B1$$

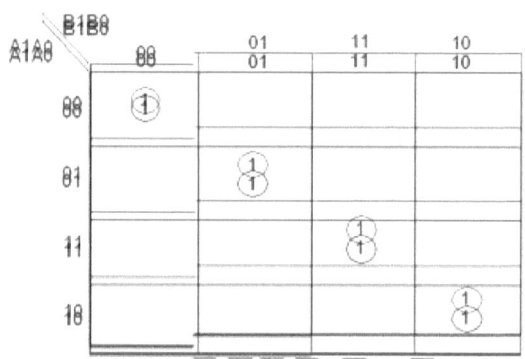

$$A \equiv B \equiv \overline{A1}\ \overline{A0}\ \overline{B1}\ \overline{B0} + \overline{A1}\ A0\ \overline{B1}\ B0 + A1\ A0\ B1\ B0 + A1\ \overline{A0}\ B1\ \overline{B0}$$

$$\equiv \overline{A1}\ \overline{B1}\ (\overline{A0}\ \overline{B0} + A0\ B0) + A1\ B1\ (A0\ B0 + \overline{A0}\ \overline{B0})$$

$$= (A0\ B0 + \overline{A0}\ \overline{B0})(A1\ B1 + \overline{A1}\ \overline{B1})$$

$$= (A0\ \text{Ex-NOR}\ B0)(A1\ \text{Ex-NOR}\ B1)$$

Therefore $A = B = (A0 \odot B0)(A1 \odot B1)$

LOGIC DIAGRAM:

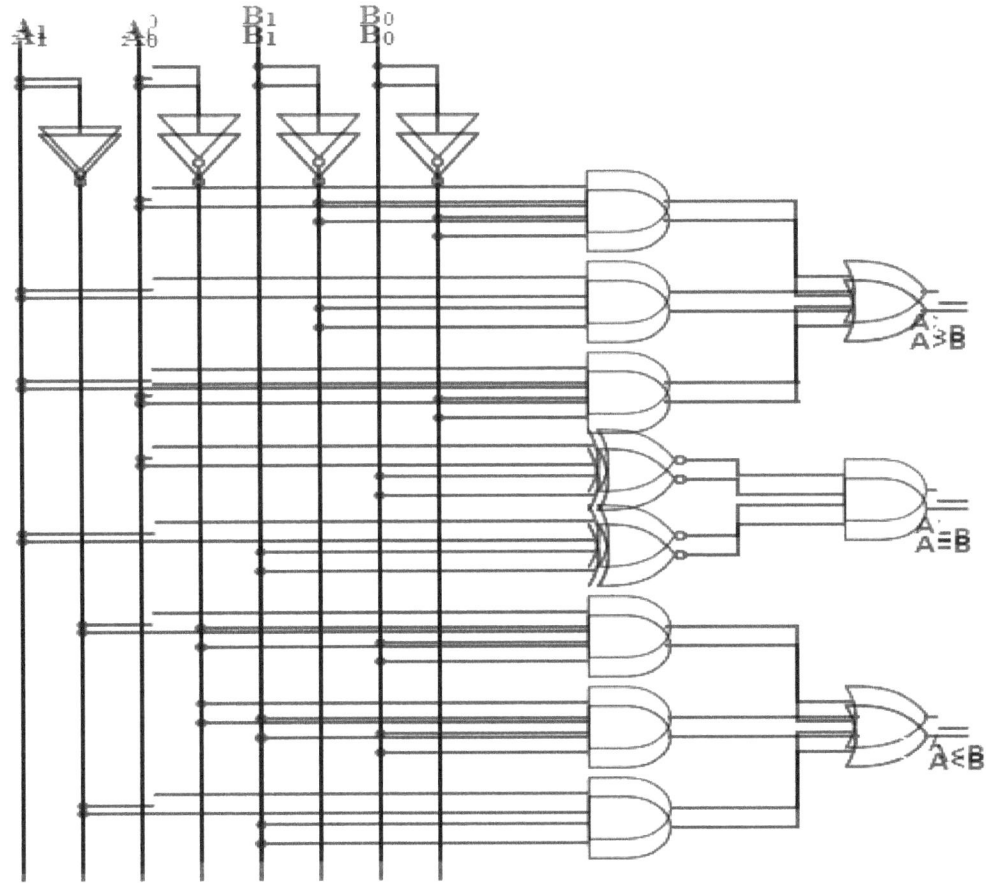

LOGISIM SIMULATION:

Step 1: For both 1-bit and 2-bit comparators draw the logic diagrams as shown above using the gates from **Gates section** and connect the inputs and output as mentioned.

OR

We can draw these comparators using simulators', **Arithmetic->Comparator section** as shown in the following snapshot. Just change the **Data Bits** as 1 or 2 in the property section of both **Input tool** and Comparator tool according to the type of comparator.

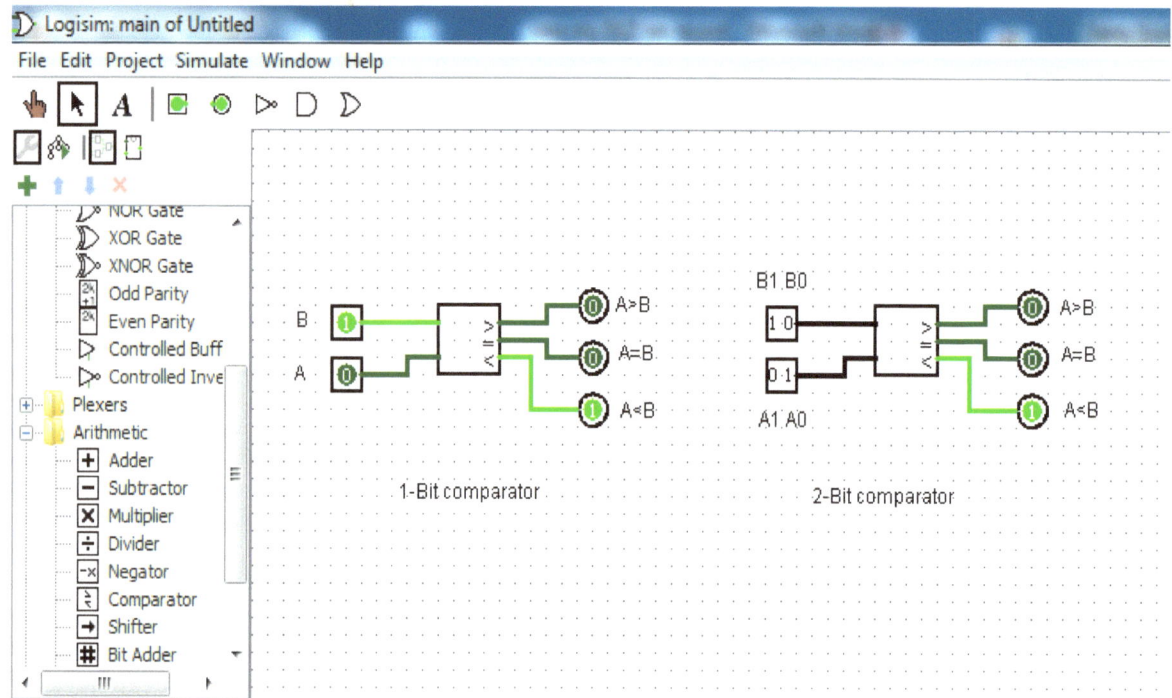

Step 2: Now use the **Toggle tool** 👆 to change the values of the inputs while observing the output. Confirm that this circuit behaves as it should as given in their Truth tables.

11. Realization of odd and even parity generation and checking.

THEORY:

A parity bit is used for detecting errors during transmission of binary information. A parity bit is an extra bit included with a binary message to make the number is either even or odd. The message including the parity bit is transmitted and then checked at the receiver ends for errors. An error is detected if the checked parity bit doesn't correspond to the one transmitted. The circuit that generates the parity bit in the transmitter is called a 'parity generator' and the circuit that checks the parity in the receiver is called a 'parity checker'.

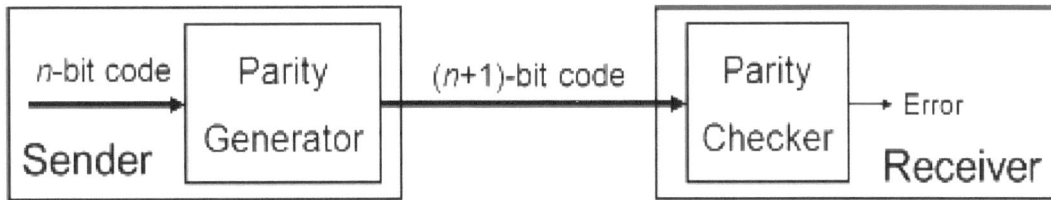

Block diagram for parity generator and checker

In even parity bit scheme, the parity bit is '0' if there are even number of 1s in the data stream and the parity bit is '1' if there are odd number of 1s in the data stream. In odd parity bit scheme, the parity bit is '1' if there are even number of 1s in the data stream and the parity bit is '0' if there are odd number of 1s in the data stream.

The parity checker circuit checks for possible errors in the transmission. If the information is passed in even parity, then the bits required must have an even number of 1's. An error occur during transmission, if the received bits have an odd number of 1's indicating that one bit has changed in value during transmission.

(1) **Even and Odd Parity Generators:**

TRUTH TABLE:

3-bit Message			Odd Parity Bit P	Even Parity Bit P
X	Y	Z		
0	0	0	1	0
0	0	1	0	1
0	1	0	0	1
0	1	1	1	0
1	0	0	0	1
1	0	1	1	0
1	1	0	1	0
1	1	1	0	1

KARNAUGH MAPS:

Boolean Expression

Even Pair
$$P = \bar{X}\bar{Y}Z + \bar{X}Y\bar{Z} + X\bar{Y}\bar{Z} + XYZ$$
$$= \bar{X}(\bar{Y}Z + Y\bar{Z}) + X(\bar{Y}\bar{Z} + YZ)$$
$$= \bar{X}(Y \oplus Z) + X(\overline{Y \oplus Z})$$
$$= X \oplus (Y \oplus Z)$$

K-Map Simplification

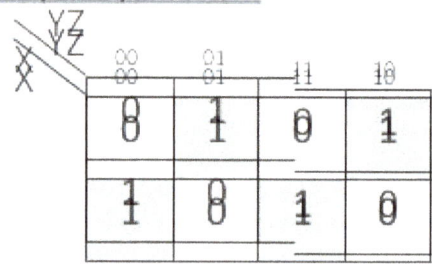

Odd Pair
$$P = \bar{X}\bar{Y}\bar{Z} + \bar{X}YZ + X\bar{Y}Z + XY\bar{Z}$$
$$= \bar{X}(\bar{Y}\bar{Z} + YZ) + X(\bar{Y}Z + Y\bar{Z})$$
$$= \bar{X}(\overline{Y \oplus Z}) + X(Y \oplus Z)$$
$$= \bar{X} \oplus (Y \oplus Z)$$

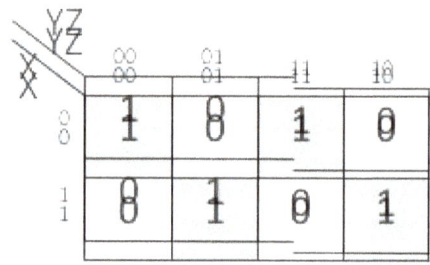

LOGIC DIAGRAMS:

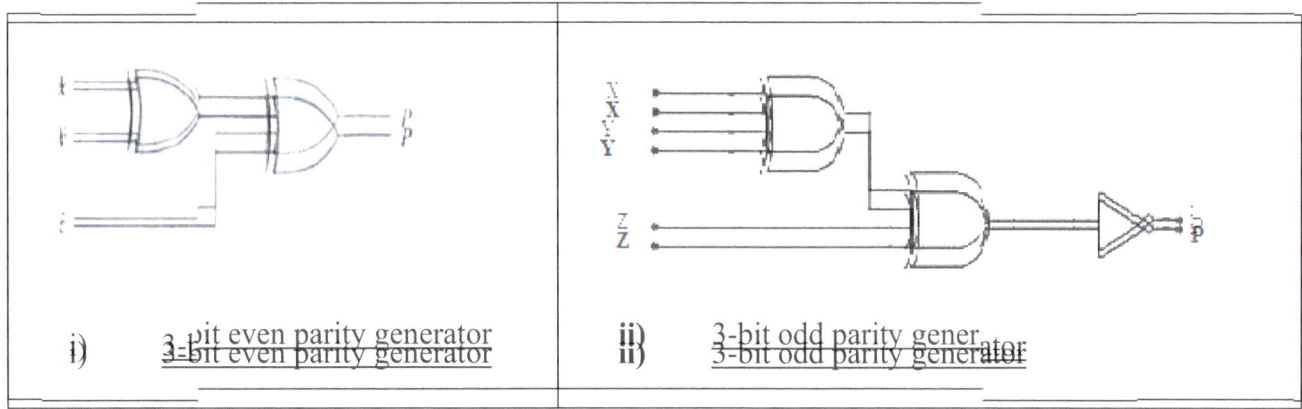

i) 3-bit even parity generator   ii) 3-bit odd parity generator

(2) Even and Odd Parity Checkers:

TRUTH TABLE:

4-bit received message				EVEN Parity error check C_p	ODD Parity error check C_p
A	B	C	P		
0	0	0	0	0	1
0	0	0	1	1	0
0	0	1	0	1	0
0	0	1	1	0	1
0	1	0	0	1	0
0	1	0	1	0	1
0	1	1	0	0	1
0	1	1	1	1	0
1	0	0	0	1	0
1	0	0	1	0	1
1	0	1	0	0	1
1	0	1	1	1	0
1	1	0	0	0	1
1	1	0	1	1	0
1	1	1	0	1	0
1	1	1	1	0	1

KARNAUGH MAPS:

Even Parity Checker:

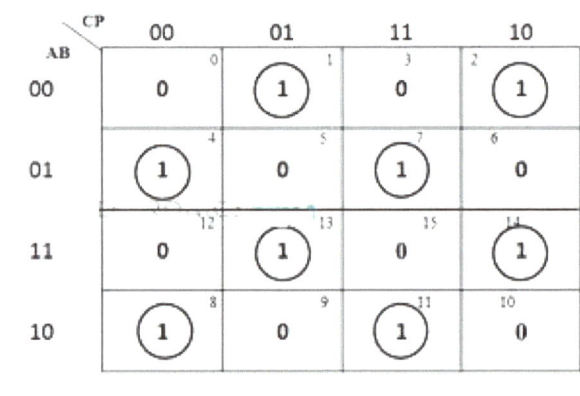

$$C_P = (A \oplus B) \oplus (C \oplus P)$$

Odd Parity Checker:

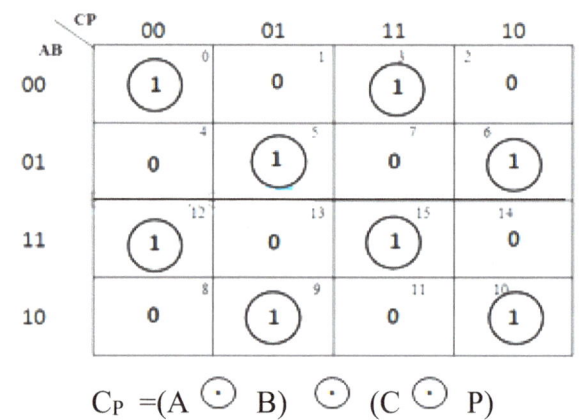

$$C_P = (A \odot B) \odot (C \odot P)$$

LOGIC DIAGRAMS:

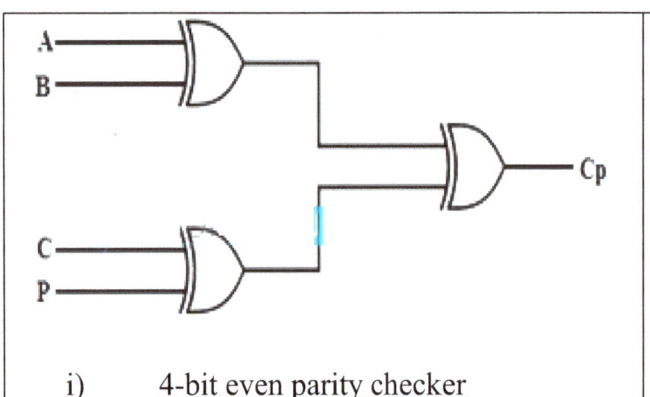

i)   4-bit even parity checker

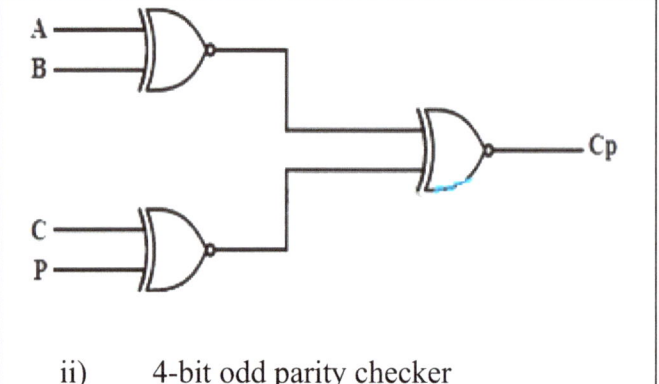

ii)   4-bit odd parity checker

LOGISIM SIMULATION:

Step 1: Draw the logic diagram as shown above using the gates from **Gates section** and connect the inputs and output as mentioned.

Step 2: Now use the **Toggle tool** 👆 to change the values of the inputs while observing the output. Confirm that this circuit behaves as it should as given in the Truth table.

REFERENCES:

1. Morris Mano M, Digital logic and computer design ,PHI.
2. Floyd and jain ,Digital Fundamentals,8/e , pearson education.
3. Alan N Marcovitz,Introduction to logic and computer design ,McGraw Hill.
4. Ronald J.Tocci,Digital Systems:Principal and applications,8/e ,pearson education.
5. Bartee J.C., Digital computer Fundamentals,6/e ,TMH.
6. Herbert Taub and Donald schilling , Digital intergrated electronics, McGraw Hill International Edition.
7. Ramesh S. Gaonkar, Microprocessor Architecture, Programming , and Application with the 8085,4/e Penram International Publishers.